AQA Psychology

GCSE

Mike Stanley

Karen Boswell

Sarah Harris

Dominic Helliwell

Joanne McKenzie

D1341614

Nelson Thornes

Published in 2009 by:
Nelson Thornes Ltd
Delta Place
27 Bath Road
CHELTENHAM
GL53 7TH
United Kingdom

11 12 13 / 10 9 8 7 6 5 4

A catalogue record for this book is available from the British Library

ISBN 978 1 4085 0395 9

Cover photograph by Getty / Chad Baker, Thomas Northcut
Illustrations by Alan Rowe, JB Illustration
Page make-up by AMR Design Ltd (www.amrdesign.com)

Printed and bound in China by 1010 Printing International Ltd

Photo Acknowledgements

Alamy: Mediscan / 1.2B; Itani Images / 1.3A; Nick Hanna / 1.3C; Yuri Arcurs / 1.3D; Angela Hampton / 1.4A; Picture Partners / 2.2C; Dave Picard / 2.2D; Mark Bourdillon / 2.2E; blickwinkel / 2.2F; Tibor Bognar / 2.2G; Kuttig - People / 2.2H; Edward Hawks / 2.2I; Zefa RF / 6.3B3; Redmond Durrell / 6.3B4; Angela Hampton / 6.4A; JoeFox / 6.4B; 67photo / 6.4D; Pictorial Press Ltd / 8.2A; Radius Images / 8.3A; Radius Images / 8.3D; Blend Images / 10.1C; Digital Vision / 10.2C; **Corbis:** Rick Gayle Studio / 5.1A; Louis Quail / 6.1D; Walter Fleischer / 6.2E; Bettmann / 6.3B1; Paul Hardy / 10.1A; **Dominic Helliwell:** 7.1B; 7.1D; 7.2C; 7.3C; 7.5A; **Fotolia:** 6.1C; 8.4E; 10.3A; **Getty Images:** Christopher Furlong / CO3; Christopher Furlong / 3.3A1; Christopher Furlong / 3.3A2; Matt Cardy / 3.3A3; Matt Cardy / 3.3A4; Ian Waldie / 5.4A; Nina Leen / Time & Life Pictures / CO6; Nina Leen / Time & Life Pictures / 6.2C; Yvonne Hemsey / 6.2D; Tom Morrison / 8.3B; David C Ellis / 8.3C; ODD ANDERSEN / AFP / 9.1C; **Howard Dully:** 9.3A; **iStockphoto:** CO1; 1.1A; 1.3B; 1.4B; 1.4C; 1.4D; CO2; 2.1A; 2.2A; 2.2B; 2.3A; 2.3B; 2.3C; 2.3D; 2.3E; 2.3F; 2.3G; 2.4A; 2.4B; 2.4C; 2.4D; 3.1E; 3.1F; 3.1G; 3.1H; 3.1I; 3.2E; 3.4B; 3.4C; CO4; 4.1B; 4.3B; 4.4B; CO5; 5.1B; 5.1C; 5.1G; 5.1H; 6.2A1; 6.2A2; 6.3B2; 6.3C; CO7; 7.3B; 7.3D; 7.4A; 7.5B; 7.6A; CO8; 8.1A; 8.1B; 8.2C; 8.4A; 8.4B; 8.4F; 8.4G; 8.4H; CO9; 9.2A; 9.3B; 9.3C; CO10; 10.1B; 10.2A; 10.2B; 10.2E; 10.2F; 10.2G; 10.4B; **Mike Stanley:** 1.2A; **PA Photos:** Joel Ryan / AP / 3.1A; Barry Coombs / EMPICS Sport / 3.1B; Suzan/Suzan / EMPICS Entertainment / 3.1C; Yui Mok / PA Archive / 3.1D; **Rex Features:** Ken McKay / 4.2A; CSU Archives / Everett Collection / 4.2B; Eye Ubiquitous / 4.3C; James McCauley / 8.2B; **Science Photo Library:** Science Source / 6.1A.

Text Acknowledgements

p. 47: List of APD characteristics reprinted with permission from the Diagnostic and Statistical Manual of Mental Disorders, Text Revision, Fourth Edition. Copyright 2000. American Psychiatric Association; p. 82-3: Mention of Code of Ethics and Conduct of the British Psychological Society 2006. Reprinted with permission; p. 124: Short extract from 'The behavioral treatment of a 'transsexual' preadolescent boy' by George. A. Rekers, O. I. Lovas, and B. P. Lowe, in JOURNAL OF ABNORMAL CHILD PSYCHOLOGY 1974, 2, 99-116. Reprinted with permission; p. 128: Figures from ChildWise Monitor Survey 2008-08. Reprinted with permission.

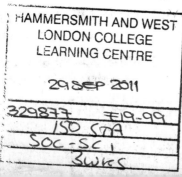

Contents

Nelson Thornes has worked in partnership with AQA to make sure that this book offers you the best possible support for your GCSE course. All the content has been approved by the senior examining team at AQA, so you can be sure that it gives you just what you need when you are preparing for your exams.

■ How to use this book

This book covers everything you need for your course.

Learning Objectives

At the beginning of each section or topic you'll find a list of Learning Objectives based on the requirements of the specification, so you can make sure you are covering everything you need to know for the exam.

> **Objectives**
> **Objectives**
> **Objectives**
> **Objectives**
> First objective.
> Second objective.

AQA Examiner's Tips

Don't forget to look at the AQA Examiner's Tips throughout the book to help you with your study and prepare for your exam.

> **AQA Examiner's tip**
> Don't forget to look at the AQA Examiner's Tips throughout the book to help you with your study and prepare for your exam.

Going further activities

These give you an opportunity to extend and stretch your knowledge and understanding of the course material.

> **Going further**
> Gain a wider understanding of the course material.

Visit **www.nelsonthornes.com/aqagcse** for more information.

What is Psychology?

The word 'psychology' comes from the combination of two Greek words, 'psyche' and 'logos'. It literally means 'the study of the mind'. However, it isn't just the mind that modern psychologists attempt to study.

When you say to people that you are studying Psychology, they will often say: 'it's all just common sense, isn't it?' But there is a lot more to it than that. Psychology is a science and we can use it to understand people's behaviour and to predict how they are likely to behave in different situations. Common sense alone is not enough and it can often contradict itself. For example, you may have heard the expression 'absence makes the heart grow fonder'. This sounds like common sense. But what about the expression 'out of sight, out of mind'? This is another bit of common sense that means exactly the opposite. You can probably think of many other examples of contradictory common sense. The job of the psychologist is to take these ideas and to test them scientifically. You are also going to discover that people will sometimes do the opposite of what common sense would predict. As you follow this course you will be amazed at what you discover about people and their behaviour.

■ AQA GCSE Psychology

AQA recognises the scientific status of Psychology. Although you are no longer required to submit a piece of coursework, the examination continues to ask candidates about the research methods used by psychologists. This textbook offers many opportunities for you to develop an understanding of research and its significance within Psychology.

The AQA GCSE Psychology specification expects you to know and understand the work of psychologists in a variety of topic areas. We firmly believe that the best way to learn Psychology is by 'hands-on' experience. You could not learn to become an expert tennis player simply by reading a textbook about tennis. You need to get onto the tennis court and try

it out; hitting the ball and playing against opponents is the best way to improve your game. Equally the best way to improve your Psychology is to try it out; practise doing Psychology! This book will give you that opportunity. Every chapter is full of activities based on the work of famous psychologists. You will be able to conduct your own research and see how your results compare to those of the psychologists. This research then becomes part of your own personal experience, which should make it easier to remember. In other words, you will be using applied psychology to help you to learn Psychology.

The Specification

Content

Unit 1 is called 'Making sense of other people'. It contains half of the information you will need to learn in the GCSE Full Course. It is also the self-contained Short Course in Psychology. This means that at the end of this unit you can take an examination that will give you a half GCSE qualification. This is a brand new qualification at GCSE level.

Unit 1 should help you to find answers to questions that have intrigued non-psychologists for years. For example:

■ Why do I forget things?

■ How can I read body language?

■ How can I tell if somebody likes me?

■ What causes Antisocial Personality Disorder?

■ What causes prejudice in the world?

Unit 2 is called 'Understanding Other People'. It is the second half of the GCSE Full Course. It will help you to find answers to other fascinating questions. For example:

■ How can I overcome a phobia?

■ How can I give up a bad habit?

■ Why are bystanders reluctant to help in emergencies?

■ What did Freud really say about sex?

■ What causes people to be so aggressive?

In both Unit 1 and Unit 2, you will learn about the research methods used by psychologists to discover answers to these questions and many more.

Assessment

Each unit will be assessed by a 90-minute question paper and each question paper will contain five questions. All of the questions are compulsory.

In each question paper, the first four questions are based on topics within the unit that you have studied and these questions are each worth 15 marks. The fifth question in each question paper is about the research methods used in Psychology and these questions are worth 20 marks. That means that each question paper is worth 80 marks. All of the questions in both papers are broken down into parts that are each worth between one and six marks. There is also a variety of question styles ranging from multiple-choice questions to short answer questions and questions that require the use of continuous prose.

When answering the exam paper, it is a good plan to think that you should be writing at the rate of approximately one mark per minute – in other words, 80 marks in 80 minutes. This then gives you roughly 10 minutes for reading and checking your answers.

Features in this book

This book contains many features to help you learn and revise effectively.

Objectives

You will find these in the margin at the beginning of each topic within a chapter. They are based on the requirements of the specification, so you can make sure you are covering everything you need to know for the exam.

Key terms

This feature provides you with definitions of all the key terms that you need to know. These are brought together in the glossary at the end of the book.

Activities

The Starter activity immediately focuses your attention on what the lesson is going to be about or lets you recap what you have learned in the previous lesson. All the other Activities are also aimed at helping you to learn actively.

Check your understanding

You will find these questions at the end of each topic within a chapter. When you answer these questions you will immediately find out whether you have understood and can remember what you have read. They are very similar to the multiple-choice and short answer questions you will meet in the exam.

Going further

Many of these activities encourage you to carry out further research on the topic, either in the classroom or at home. In some cases, suggestions are made about websites to use. These research activities will help to broaden your knowledge of the topic.

Did you know

These provide short sharp snippets of information.

Links

If there is relevant information in a different part of the book you will find a link to it in the margin.

Examiner's tips

Don't forget to look at the AQA Examiner's tips throughout the book. They will give you an insight into what examiners expect as well as pitfalls to avoid.

1 Memory

1.1 What is the multi-store explanation of memory processes?

1 How good is your memory? Take a minute to complete this questionnaire. On a separate piece of paper, write down each answer that is correct for you. Be honest!

How often do you forget each of these? Choose from Never, Sometimes, Often and Always.

a   Birthdays

b   People's names

c   Returning things you borrowed

d   Where you put something

e   What you went into a room for

f   Telephone numbers

g   Information for tests

h   Doing homework

Use this scoring system: Never = 0, Sometimes = 1, Often = 2, Always = 3. What is your total score? It should be between 0 and 24. The higher your score, the worse you think your memory is.

Objectives

You will be able to:

understand the flow of information in memory

understand the distinction between encoding, storage and retrieval

understand the multi-store explanation of memory

suggest practical applications of the multi-store explanation of memory.

■ Flow of information in memory

Our memory is a bit like a video or DVD recorder. Basically there are three things (known as processes) that we need to do: put information in, keep it there until we need it, and then get it back. Putting information in is called **encoding**. To do this, information is changed to a language or code that the brain will understand. Keeping it there until we need it is called **storage**. We can store vast amounts of information, some of it for a lifetime. However, for this process to work properly, we need to be able to find the information when we need it. Bringing information back out of storage is called **retrieval**. The flow of information in memory is presented in Diagram **B**.

Key terms

Encoding: changing information so that it can be stored.

Storage: holding information in the memory system.

Retrieval: recovering information from storage.

Multi-store: the idea that information passes through a series of memory stores.

Sensory store: holds information received from the senses for a very short period of time.

Short-term store: holds approximately seven chunks of information for a limited amount of time.

Long-term store: holds a vast amount of information for a very long period of time.

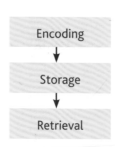

Encoding
↓
Storage
↓
Retrieval

A *Memory is a bit like a video or DVD recorder*

B *The flow of information in memory*

Activity

1   Here is a list of the planets that orbit the Sun, shown in the correct order:

Mercury   Venus   Earth   Mars   Jupiter   Saturn   Uranus   Neptune   Pluto

Find someone who does not know the correct order and give them 30 seconds to learn the list. Then wait for another 60 seconds and ask them to recite the list. How did they do?

Now find someone else who doesn't know the correct order and show them the information below for 30 seconds.

| Mercury | Venus | Earth | Mars | Jupiter | Saturn | Uranus | Neptune | Pluto |
| My | Very | Easy | Method | Just | Speeds | Up | Naming | Planets |

Wait 60 seconds and ask them to recite the list of planets in the correct order. How did they do?

This activity is about encoding, storage and retrieval. Can you identify the encoding method, how long the information was stored and who did the best retrieval?

One explanation of memory says that it has more than one store. This is called the **multi-store** explanation. Information arrives at our senses (sight, sound, taste, touch, smell). This is briefly held in a part of our memory known as the **sensory store**. But it only stays there for a very short period of time and it will quickly fade away if we don't do something with it.

Activity 2 demonstrates that there is another memory store known as the **short-term store**. Experiments have shown that this store has a small capacity. It can hold approximately seven items or 'chunks' of information. New information pushes old information out. That is why your partner for Activity 2 probably had trouble recalling more than seven numbers. Also, if you do not rehearse the information, it will probably be forgotten within a minute or so.

Activities

2   Find a partner and ask them to recall out loud things that you say to them. For this activity, it is better to work with numbers. Keep it simple to begin with and ask them to recall a single digit number. For example, say '7, recall'. That's easy! Now give them two digits to recall: '6, 3, recall'. Still pretty easy. Keep doing this, adding one more digit each time. How long can they go before they make a mistake? If they go beyond seven digits they have done very well.

3   Select 15 seven-letter words from a dictionary and then write each one on a separate piece of card. Find a few willing volunteers and show them the words one at a time, for about two seconds for each card. Wait for one minute and then ask your volunteers to write down as many words as they can remember in any order they like. Give them no more than two minutes to do this. Which words did they recall?

The prediction is that they recalled more of the first few and the last few words and not many of the words from the middle.

Activity 3 shows that there is a third memory store known as the **long-term store**. Experiments have shown that this store has a very large capacity and information can stay there indefinitely.

So, let's look more closely at this multi-store explanation, beginning on the next page.

Did you know ??????

People usually can recall fewer than 10 per cent of the names of people they have met even though they can recognise their faces.

2 How much can you remember so far? Without looking back, write down what is meant by the following terms:

a encoding   b storage   c retrieval.

■ Multi-store explanation of memory

Atkinson and Shiffrin (1968) thought that information passes through a series of memory stores and each of these stores has different characteristics, as you have already seen. The activities you have just done help us to understand the multi-store explanation of memory. The flow of information through the multi-store memory is shown in Diagram **C**.

C *Flow of information through the multi-store memory*

Memory store	Duration	Capacity
Sensory	Less than one second	Very limited
Short-term	Less than one minute	Approximately seven chunks of information
Long-term	Up to a lifetime	Unlimited

D *Duration and capacity of each memory store*

When you want to learn a list of words, it starts as a visual image in the sensory store. Then you will probably try saying them to yourself (rehearsal) as they move to the short-term store. If you are successful, the words will move to the long-term store and you will be able to recall them later.

Research study

Peterson and Peterson (1959)

Aim: To see if rehearsal was necessary to hold information in the short-term store.

Method: Participants were given sets of three letters to remember (such as GYK, MTW), but were immediately asked to count backwards in threes out loud for different lengths of time. This was done to prevent rehearsal. Participants were then asked to recall the letters in the correct order.

Results: The results of the study showed that participants had forgotten virtually all of the information after 18 seconds.

Conclusion: It was concluded that we cannot hold information in the short-term store unless we can rehearse it.

Research study

Research study: Murdock (1962)

Aim: To provide evidence to support the multi-store explanation of memory.

Method: Participants had to learn a list of words presented one at a time, for two seconds per word, and then recall the words in any order.

Key terms

Recency effect: information received later is recalled better than earlier information.

Primacy effect: the first information received is recalled better than subsequent information.

Results: The words at the end of the list were recalled first (known as the **recency effect**). Words from the beginning of the list were also recalled quite well (known as the **primacy effect**), but the middle words were not recalled very well at all.

Conclusion: Murdock concluded that this provides evidence for separate short-term and long-term stores.

Murdock claimed that the recency effect is evidence that the last few words were still in the short-term store. The primacy effect is evidence that the first few words flowed into the long-term store.

Evaluation

For Activity 1, you may have said that participants in the studies described only had to learn nonsense syllables or lists of words. These are not the type of memory tasks that people usually have to do in the real world. Therefore, the studies lack ecological validity.

You might have said that not everything we learn has to be rehearsed. Many everyday events are easily remembered. It is also true that saying things over and over does not necessarily make them easier to recall. It is more important to understand the meaning of information so that you can say it in your own words.

However, the studies help us to understand why it is so difficult to remember the registration number of a passing car or someone's telephone number. Therefore, we should not just dismiss this explanation of memory as incorrect.

Activity

5 If the multi-store explanation is correct, what are its practical applications? Work with partners to think of at least **two** practical applications of the multi-store explanation in everyday life. Don't read on until you have attempted this activity.

Practical applications

Knowing that the capacity of the short-term store is approximately seven 'chunks' of information, you may have realised why car registration numbers never exceed that number. Therefore, if you need to remember a registration number, you have a chance of doing so by saying it over and over to yourself.

It is the same with postcodes. How many letters and numbers are in your postcode?

Check your understanding

1 Outline what is meant by the term 'encoding'. *(2 marks)*

2 Identify and describe **three** features of the multi-store explanation of memory. *(6 marks)*

3 Describe **one** study in which the multi-store explanation of memory was investigated. *(4 marks)*

4 Outline **one** practical application of the multi-store explanation of memory. *(2 marks)*

Activity

4 What do you think of the studies of Peterson and Peterson, and Murdock?

Work with a partner to try to think of at least **three** criticisms (evaluations). These don't all have to be negative; you might have positive things to say about them. Don't read on until you have attempted this activity.

⬯links

See Topic 5.1 on page 74 for more information about the term 'ecological validity'.

Going further

Working with a partner, try to replicate Murdock's study using different variations. For example, you could use lists of words of different lengths, such as 20, 30 and 40 words. How strong is the evidence of the primacy and recency effects for each of these lists? What happens if you vary the presentation times for the words in these lists? In the study described in this chapter, words were presented at two seconds per word. Try one second per word. Does this make a difference?

AQA Examiner's tip

When you are asked to identify a feature, this means that you must name it. You would get one mark for that. Then, to describe it, you must say something more about that feature.

Starter activity

1   What can you remember about the multi-store explanation of memory?

Name **three** memory stores and identify **two** characteristics of each.

Can you do this within five minutes?

A   'Chinese whispers'

Objectives

You will be able to:

understand the reconstructive explanation of memory

understand the levels of processing explanation of memory

suggest practical applications of these explanations of memory.

Reconstructive memory

Bartlett (1932) thought that memory was not just a stored copy of facts. He said that we change our memories to fit in with what we already know, even though we think we are remembering exactly what happened. This is known as **reconstructive memory**.

Research study

Bartlett (1932)

Aim: To see if people, when given something unfamiliar to remember, would alter the information.

Method: Participants were asked to read a story called 'The War of the Ghosts', which was a Native American legend. Later they were asked to retell the story as accurately as possible. This retelling was repeated several times during the weeks that followed.

Results: Bartlett discovered that his participants found it difficult to remember bits of the story concerned with spirits and changed other bits of the story so that it made more sense to them. Each time they retold the story they changed it some more.

Conclusion: Bartlett concluded that our memory is influenced by our own beliefs.

Activity

1   Have you ever played 'Chinese whispers'? Write a short and simple message, about 10 to 15 words long. Get a few of your group to stand in a line about one metre apart. Now whisper your message into the ear of the first person in the line. They should then whisper the message to the next person, and so on down the line until the message reaches the last person. Ask that person to say the message out loud.

How does it compare with your original message? The chances are that it will be quite different. Why?

Key terms

Reconstructive memory: altering our recollection of things so that they make more sense to us.

When you did Activity 1, the other people in your group probably thought they were passing on your message accurately. Without knowing, they actually changed it so that it made more sense to them.

A more recent study was conducted by Wynn and Logie (1998).

Research study

Wynn and Logie (1998)

Aim: To see if the recall of familiar stories changed in the same way that Bartlett found with unfamiliar stories.

Method: They asked university students to recall details of their first week at university. They were asked to do this several times throughout the year.

Results: The results showed that the accuracy of their descriptions remained the same no matter how many times they were asked to recall the information. This is unlike Bartlett's participants who changed their stories with every telling.

Conclusion: Wynn and Logie concluded that memories for familiar events will not change over time.

Activity

2 What do you think of the studies of reconstructive memory that have been described? Working with a partner, try to think of at least **three** criticisms (evaluations). Don't read on until you have attempted this activity.

Evaluation

The reconstructive explanation is important because it emphasises the influence of people's previous knowledge and background on the way they remember things. Perhaps this is why people of different cultures have difficulty in agreeing with each other.

You may have criticised the studies because it would be very difficult to measure the accuracy of the stories told with a reliable scoring method. Bartlett's story 'War of the Ghosts' is confusing and not similar to our everyday experiences. Wynn and Logie's participants may not have changed their stories during the year but how do we know how accurate they were to begin with? There would have been no independent way of checking that.

However, you may also think that these studies are more relevant to the way we use our memories in everyday life. We often tell people about what others have said to us. When you are telling someone about your day, do you emphasise some things and play down other things? This is what reconstructive memory is all about.

Practical applications

This explanation of memory helps us to understand why two people who are recalling the same event might have completely different versions of the story. It does not necessarily mean that one of them is lying. They each might genuinely believe that their version of the story is accurate.

The reconstructive explanation also teaches us that we must be very careful giving or listening to eyewitness accounts of events such as accidents or crimes. Witnesses might think they are being accurate but, in trying to make sense of what they saw, alter the facts. We shall deal with this issue later on in this chapter.

Going further

1 Working with a partner, try to replicate Bartlett's study using participants from your own community.

■ Find the story 'War of the Ghosts' on the internet (there is a link from the BBC web page: www.bbc.co.uk/radio4/science/mindchangers3.shtml).

■ Design an experiment to see how the telling of the story changes over time. You will have to devise a clever scoring technique.

links

See Topic 5.1 for help in designing an experiment.

Activity

3 Now that you know about the reconstructive explanation of memory, what practical applications can you think of? Work with your partner and try to think of at least **two** practical applications.

Did you know ??????

When people are asked to estimate how many things they remember each day, they usually say between 100 and 10,000. The actual answer is closer to many millions. Every moment of the day our memories are helping us to make sense of everything that is happening around us.

2 Without looking back, outline the reconstructive explanation of memory. Try not to take longer than three minutes to do this.

Levels of processing

Activity

4 Do this activity on your own and ask everybody in your group to do the same.

On a separate piece of paper, answer the questions below by choosing either '**yes**' or '**no**'. Do this as quickly as possible.

a   Is this word written in lower case?   CLEAR

b   Does this word rhyme with door?   floor

c   Is this word the name of an animal?   TIGER

d   Is this word the name of a disease?   table

e   Is this word written in upper case?   PROUD

f   Does this word rhyme with cheek?   brush

g   Is this word written in lower case?   FLAME

h   Does this word rhyme with power?   flour

i   Is this something to wear?   DRESS

j   Does this word rhyme with cove?   drove

k   Is this word written in upper case?   FIELD

l   Is this a type of fruit?   apple

Now cover everything on this page and in one minute write down as many of the 12 words that you can remember.

Don't cheat!

Check which words you recalled correctly. If you can, also check which words others in your group recalled correctly. Count how many times each word was recalled.

If the last activity went according to plan, the prediction is that the following words were recalled well: 'tiger', 'table', 'dress' and 'apple'. You probably recalled fewer of these words: 'floor', 'brush', 'flour' and 'drove'. You may have recalled even fewer of these words: 'clear', 'proud', 'flame' and 'field'. Why do you think this happened?

According to Craik and Lockhart (1972), it is the way you think about information (or process it) that is important if you want to recall it later. We can think about information, such as words, at different levels. At a shallow level, known as **structural processing**, we look at visual features of words, such as whether they are written in upper-case or lower-case letters. At a middle level, known as **phonetic processing**, we think about the sound of words. At a deep level, known as **semantic processing**, we think about the meanings of words.

Key terms

Structural processing: thinking about the physical appearance of words to be learnt.

Phonetic processing: thinking about the sound of words to be learnt.

Semantic processing: thinking about the meaning of words to be learnt.

Levels of processing: the depth at which information is thought about when trying to learn it.

Did you know ??????

Brain scans show:

- high levels of brain activity when you think about the *meaning* of words
- less activity when you think about the *sounds* of words
- even less activity when you think about the *structure* of words.

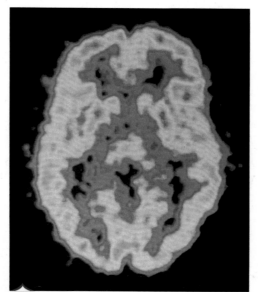

B   *PET scan of a normal brain*

Research study

Craik and Lockhart (1972)

Aim: To see if the type of question asked about words will have an effect on the number of words recalled.

Method: Participants were presented with a list of words, one at a time, and asked questions about each word, to which they had to answer 'yes' or 'no'. Some questions required structural processing of the words; others required phonetic processing and the remainder required semantic processing. They were then given a longer list of words and asked to identify the words they had answered questions about.

Results: Participants identified 70 per cent of the words that required semantic processing, 35 per cent of the words that required phonetic processing and 15 per cent of the words that required structural processing.

Conclusion: The more deeply information is processed, the more likely it is to be remembered.

Activity

5   What do you think of the **levels of processing** study that has been described? Working with a partner, try to think of at least **three** criticisms (evaluations). Don't read on until you have attempted this activity.

Evaluation

Craik and Lockhart's study has been criticised because it does not explain why deeper levels of processing helps memory. Some people have said that deeper processing takes more time and that is what helps us to recall more information. Deeper processing also takes more effort and perhaps it is the extra effort that helps us. You may also have said something about the ecological validity of the study because real-life memory tasks are not usually about learning lists of words.

Activity

6   Now that you know about the levels of processing explanation of memory, what practical applications can you think of? Work with a partner and try to think of at least **two** practical applications. Don't read on until you have attempted this activity.

Practical applications

One obvious application would be to improve study skills. Instead of just reading something over and over in the hope that you might remember it better, try reading it once and then writing it down in your own words. Doing it this way requires semantic processing.

Going further

2   Work with a group of students to create a poster to compare the three explanations of memory that you have learnt so far. The poster could include key features of each explanation, how long-term memories are created or how they relate to real-life experiences. You might be able to think of other comparisons too. The poster could be in the form of a grid or spider diagram or some other imaginative way of comparing the explanations.

AQA Examiner's tip

When you are asked to describe a study, you must always state the aim of the study, the method used, the results obtained and the conclusion drawn. You must include all four elements in your answer to receive all of the marks.

Check your understanding

1   Outline the levels of processing explanation of memory. *(4 marks)*

2   Describe **one** study in which the reconstructive explanation of memory was investigated. *(4 marks)*

3   Outline **one** practical application of the levels of processing explanation of memory. *(2 marks)*

1.3 Why do we forget?

Objectives

You will be able to:

understand how interference can affect memory

understand how context can affect memory

understand how brain damage can affect memory

suggest practical applications derived from explanations of forgetting.

Starter activity

1   What causes us to forget things?

Try to think of an occasion when you just could not recall something you thought you knew.

What do you think might have caused that to happen? Write down your ideas.

Activity

1   Work with a partner and make 10 copies of each of these word lists.

List 1: paper, lettuce, table, picture, drawer, sailor, floor, thought, feature, until.

List 2: pencil, cabbage, chair, portrait, cupboard, soldier, ceiling, idea, activity, before.

Find 10 willing participants and give them one minute to learn the words in List 1. Now give the same 10 participants one minute to learn List 2. Wait one minute; give them each a blank piece of paper and give them another minute to recall the words from List 1. How did they do?

Now find another 10 participants and give them one minute to learn the words in List 1. Wait two minutes; give them a blank piece of paper and ask them to recall the words from List 1. How did they do? Better than your first group of participants? Did members of your first group write down any words from List 2?

A   'I knew it yesterday, but I just cannot recall it now!'

The prediction is that your second group of participants recalled more words correctly than your first group. This is probably because List 2 acted as **interference** for the first group.

Key terms

Interference: things that we have learnt that make it difficult to recall other information that we have learnt.

Retroactive interference: when information we have recently learnt hinders our ability to recall information we have learnt previously.

Proactive interference: when information we have already learnt hinders our ability to recall new information.

Interference

New things that we learn can cause problems when we try to recall information that we learned before. This is known as **retroactive interference**.

Research study

Underwood and Postman (1960)

Aim: To see if new learning interferes with previous learning.

Method: Participants were divided into two groups:

- Group A were asked to learn a list of word pairs (cat–tree, candle–table, apple–lake). They were then asked to learn a second list of word pairs (cat–glass, candle–whale, apple–sadness).
- Group B were asked to learn the first list of word pairs only.

Both groups were asked to recall the first list of word pairs.

Results: Group B's recall of the first list was more accurate than that of Group A.

Conclusion: New learning interfered with participants' ability to recall the first list.

Underwood and Postman thought that retroactive interference will be worse when there is a strong similarity between old and new information to be learned.

It has also been found that things that we already know can cause problems when we try to take in new information. This is known as **proactive interference**. Now do Activity 2.

You probably realised that for Activity 2, Group B would learn the second list and that both groups would have to recall the second list.

Activity

3 Now that you know how interference can affect memory, what practical applications can you think of for this knowledge? Working with a partner, try to think of at least **two** practical applications. Also try to think of benefits and drawbacks that go with this.

You may have said that a practical application could be in developing better study habits. If you have more than one subject to revise in a particular evening, try to avoid studying two subjects that are similar, for example two different languages or two sciences. Or if you do have to study similar subjects, try to put some space between study sessions by taking a break.

However, do not just think about study habits. How about activities such as sports? Skills learned for one sport might interfere with developing skills for a different sport, such as learning to play both tennis and badminton.

Activity

2 a Working with a partner, design an experiment to investigate proactive interference. (Hint: in some ways this could look quite similar to Underwood and Postman's experiment.)

b If you have time, try to conduct this experiment using other members of your group as participants.

B *Trying to learn two similar things at the same time could cause interference*

Did you know ??????

An American psychologist who spent years studying brain cells and their capacity for storage said that if we fed into a human brain 10 items of information per second for an entire lifetime, the brain would be less than half full.

Starter activity

2 Without looking back, spend two minutes writing down what you think the difference is between proactive interference and retroactive interference.

■ Context

Have you ever gone to another room for something and then, when you got there, forgot why you were there? Then, when you returned to where you started from, did you remember why you went? This happens to a lot of people. Why do you think this happens?

Activity

4 For this activity you need a partner to work with and you will also need to make another word list. Using a dictionary, select 20 words at random and write them as a list on a sheet of paper. You will need to make enough copies of this list for every member of your group.

Now hand the word list to every member of your group and give them two minutes to try to learn it. After that, collect in the word lists and divide the group into two smaller groups. Take one of these groups to another room or out into the corridor. Give them two minutes to write down, in silence, all the words they can recall. At the same time, your partner should ask the other group, who are still in the room, to do the same thing.

Compare the performance of both groups. Did one group recall more words than the other group?

The prediction is that the group left in the room will have recalled more words on average. Why do you think this happens?

Key terms

Context: the general setting or environment in which activities happen.

Anterograde amnesia: being unable to learn new information after suffering brain damage.

Hippocampus: a brain structure that is crucial for memory.

Retrograde amnesia: loss of memory for events that happened before brain damage occurred.

Research study

Godden and Baddeley (1975)

Aim: To see if people who learn and are tested in the same environment will recall more information than those who learn and are tested in different environments.

Method: Participants were deep-sea divers. They were divided into four groups. All of the groups were given the same list of words to learn:

- Group 1 had to learn underwater and recall underwater.
- Group 2 had to learn underwater and recall on the shore.
- Group 3 had to learn on the shore and recall on the shore.
- Group 4 had to learn on the shore and recall underwater.

Results: Groups 1 and 3 recalled 40 per cent more words than Groups 2 and 4.

Conclusion: Recall of information will be better if it happens in the same **context** that learning takes place.

C Learning underwater

D Learning on the shore

Activity

5 Now that you know how context can affect memory, what practical applications can you think of for this knowledge? Working with a partner, try to think of at least **two** practical applications. Also try to think of benefits and drawbacks of this.

You might have said that it would be better to take examinations in the same room where the information was learnt. Unfortunately, you do not usually have lessons in the examination hall. However, you could make your learning environment at home resemble the environment in which you are tested. For example, always work at a desk rather than spreading your books around on your bed. It would probably be a good idea not to study with music on in the background because there will not be music in the examination hall.

Brain damage and forgetting

Some people suffer brain damage and are then unable to learn new information. This is known as **anterograde amnesia**.

Miller (1968)

A patient suffering from epilepsy underwent an operation in which two-thirds of his **hippocampus** was removed. Since the operation he was unable to learn new information. This shows that the hippocampus is crucial for recording new memories.

Other people have suffered brain damage that has left them unable to recall anything that happened before the damage occurred. This is known as **retrograde amnesia**.

Russell and Nathan (1946)

A 22-year-old patient had fallen from his motorcycle, banged his head and suffered severe concussion. Although X-rays showed no fracture of the skull, he could not recall any events that had happened for two years prior to the accident.

Case studies

Did you know ???????

If you are learning something and there happens to be a particular fragrance in the air at the time, later on if you smell that fragrance again it will trigger the memory of what you were learning. This could happen even years later.

Going further

Now that you know some of the causes of forgetting, you should be able to use this knowledge to suggest ways to improve your memory.

Working with a partner, create a poster entitled 'Improve Your Memory'.

Do some extra research to find out if there are other reasons for forgetting too.

Check your understanding

1 Explain what is meant by the term 'retrograde amnesia'. *(3 marks)*

2 Describe **one study** in which the effect of interference on memory was investigated. *(4 marks)*

3 Using your knowledge of psychology, explain **one** practical application derived from explanations of memory and forgetting. *(3 marks)*

AQA Examiner's tip

When you are asked to describe a study, it is not necessary to remember the name of the psychologist who conducted the study. No marks are given for this. However, the description of the study must be accurate.

1.4 How accurate are eyewitness testimonies?

Starter activity

1 Divide into groups of three or four. Decide on a recent event that you all remember. It could be what happened at morning registration or an item in the news.

Now each write down everything you can remember about that event. Most importantly, do it independently! Don't look at what someone else is writing.

Compare what each of you has written and make a list of similarities and differences between your accounts. Did you all completely agree with each other? Were there any surprising differences?

Objectives

You will be able to:

identify factors that affect the reliability of eyewitness testimony

describe and evaluate studies of these factors

suggest practical applications derived from studies of eyewitness testimony.

It is often found that, when several people describe an event that they have all experienced, their accounts can be quite different from each other. This can be worrying in certain situations. For example, if people have witnessed an accident or a crime, how accurate will their descriptions be? They may be asked to give evidence in court. Someone might be convicted on the strength of that evidence. Witnesses might feel very confident about what they have seen. However, research has shown that, even if witnesses are confident, it does not mean that their accounts of what they saw are accurate.

A *If questioned later, how accurately could you describe this scene?*

Did you know ?????

Experiments have shown that, no matter what nationality they are, people are much better at recognising the faces of individuals from their own ethnic background than those from other ethnic backgrounds.

Activity

1 Working with a partner, try to think of at least **three** factors that might affect the **reliability** of eyewitness accounts. Don't read ahead until you have attempted this activity.

■ Factors affecting eyewitness accounts

In responding to Activity 1, you may have said something about the way people are asked questions about what they witnessed.

Key terms

Reliability: in the context of eyewitness testimony, the extent to which it can be regarded as accurate.

Leading question: a question that hints that a particular type of answer is required.

Cognitive interview: a method of questioning witnesses that involves recreating the context of an event.

Leading questions

Loftus and Palmer (1974)

Aim: To see if asking **leading questions** affect the accuracy of recall.

Method: Participants were shown films of car accidents. Some were asked 'How fast was the car going when it *hit* the other car?' Others were asked 'How fast was the car going when it *smashed* the other car?'

Results: Those who heard the word 'smashed' gave a higher speed estimate than those who heard 'hit'.

Conclusion: Leading questions will affect the accuracy of recall. The word 'smashed' led participants to believe the car was going faster.

B *How fast was the car going when it hit the van?*

Unfamiliar faces

Bruce and Young (1998)

Aim: To see if familiarity affects the accuracy of identifying faces.

Method: Psychology lecturers were caught on security cameras at the entrance of a building. Participants were asked to identify the faces seen on the security camera tape from a series of high-quality photographs.

Results: The lecturers' students made more correct identifications than other students and experienced police officers.

Conclusion: Previous familiarity helps when identifying faces.

Going further

1 Working with a partner, try to find evidence for other factors that may affect the reliability of eyewitness accounts of people and incidents. You can use other textbooks, journals and the internet to do your research.

Present your findings to the rest of your group.

Context

Geiselman *et al.* (1985)

Aim: To see if reinstating the context of an event will affect the accuracy of witnesses' accounts.

Method: Participants were shown a police training film of a violent crime. Two days later they were interviewed about what they had seen. For half of the participants, the context of the event was recreated during the interview. For the other half of the participants, standard police interview techniques were used.

Results: The participants who had the context recreated recalled more accurate facts about the violent crime than the other participants.

Conclusion: Recreating context during interviews will increase the accuracy of recall. This method is known as the **cognitive interview**.

∞ links

Geiselman's study is supported by Godden & Baddeley's study of the effect of context on memory described on page 18 in Topic 1.3.

Starter activity

2 Without looking back, write down **three** factors that affect the reliability of eyewitness testimony.

Activity

2 What do you think of the studies of eyewitness accounts of people and incidents that have been described? Working with a partner, try to think of at least **three** evaluations. Don't read on until you have attempted this activity.

Key terms

Stereotype: an oversimplified, generalised set of ideas that we have about others, for example, secondary head teachers are strict, intimidating, scary and male.

Evaluation

You might have said that watching a film or a video of an event is not the same as a real-life experience. This is because when you are watching a film you are prepared for what is about to happen and you are in a safe environment. If you witness a real-life incident, you are not usually expecting it to happen, so it takes you by surprise. Also, the situation might pose some danger for you. All this could have an effect on what you are able to recall.

However, Bruce and Young's experiment does demonstrate the limited value of security cameras when it comes to identifying someone.

There are other factors that could cause eyewitness testimony to be unreliable. The length of time between the incident and the time that witnesses were questioned might be important, as memory fades over time. Our emotional state at the time of the incident may also affect our ability to recall accurately. **Stereotypes** that we hold may also influence our recall.

Did you know ??????

Although eyewitness testimony has been found to be only 60 per cent reliable, it is admissible in courts of law. On the other hand, even though lie detector evidence has been found to be 80 per cent reliable, at present it is not admissible in British courts of law.

Research study

Cohen (1981)

Aim: To see if stereotypes can affect memory.

Method: Participants were shown a video of a man and a woman eating in a restaurant. Half of the participants were told that the woman was a waitress. The other participants were told she was a librarian. Later, all the participants were asked to describe the woman's behaviour and personality.

Results: The two groups of participants gave entirely different descriptions, which matched the stereotypes of a waitress or a librarian.

Conclusion: Stereotypes affect the accuracy of accounts of people.

C *Waitress or librarian?*

Activity

3 Now that you know about factors that can affect the reliability of eyewitness accounts of people and incidents, what practical applications can you think of for this knowledge? Working with a partner, try to think of at least **two** practical applications. Also try to think of benefits and drawbacks that go with this. Don't read on until you have attempted this activity.

⚬⚬ links

See Topic 4.1 for more information about stereotypes.

Practical applications

We know from the Loftus and Palmer study that leading questions can change memory. Therefore, when talking to witnesses, police and lawyers should avoid asking leading questions and should adopt a neutral style of questioning.

From the Bruce and Young study, we know that memory for faces can be unreliable in certain situations. Therefore, we should realise that identity parades alone might have limited use when trying to find a suspected criminal, especially when witnesses are asked to identify a stranger. There needs to be other evidence as well.

The Geiselman study shows us the importance of context when trying to accurately recall an incident. Therefore, taking witnesses back to the scene of the incident may help their recall. It would also help if the interviewer and person being interviewed tried to recreate the context in which the incident occurred (this could include the surroundings, weather conditions and how the witness was feeling), before the witness tries to recall the events themselves.

D   *Returning to the scene of an incident helps to restore context*

Going further

2   Now that you have covered everything you need to know about memory for this course, create a spider diagram that links all this knowledge together.

Do this activity with a partner. Then see which pair in your group has produced the most organised and helpful spider diagram.

AQA Examiner's tip

Remember that when a six-mark question asks you to 'describe and evaluate' a study, three marks are for the description of the study and three marks are for the evaluation.

Check your understanding

1   Outline **one** factor that affects the reliability of eyewitness accounts of people and incidents. *(2 marks)*

2   Describe and evaluate **one** study conducted by Loftus in which eyewitness testimony was investigated. *(6 marks)*

3   Outline **two** practical applications derived from studies of eyewitness testimony. *(4 marks)*

2 Non-verbal communication

2.1 How do we communicate?

Starter activity

We are all familiar with the word **communication**, but how would you define it? Take two minutes to write down what you think would be a good definition for 'communication'.

Activity

1 Working in a small group, make a list of at least **10** different ways that people communicate with each other. One thing that you should not put on your list is 'body language'. Be more specific than that.

Which group can create the longest list?

When you have completed your list, rearrange it into three columns with these headings: 'Communicating with words', 'Communicating without words' and 'Communicating using technology'.

There are many ways that people communicate; the list is almost endless. In your list you have probably included things such as email, texting, social networking websites, and many others that use technology. However, in this chapter we are more concerned with ways that we communicate without the use of technology.

Communication that requires the use of words or vocal sounds is called **verbal communication**, for example talking to someone or even just grunting. This also includes **paralinguistics**. These are vocal features that accompany speech, such as **tone of voice**, **emphasis** or **intonation**.

Communication that does not require the use of words or vocal sounds is called **non-verbal communication**. This includes eye contact, facial expressions and body language, which will be dealt with later on in this chapter. Now do Activity 2.

A *It is not just the words that are important in conversation*

Objectives

You will be able to:

understand the distinction between non-verbal and verbal communication

describe and evaluate studies of verbal communication.

Key terms

Communication: passing information from one person to another.

Verbal communication: conveying messages using words or vocal sounds.

Paralinguistics: vocal features that accompany speech.

Tone of voice: the way words are spoken to convey emotion.

Emphasis: giving prominence to some words more than others.

Intonation: inflection in the voice when speaking.

Non-verbal communication: conveying messages that do not require the use of words or vocal sounds.

Activity

2 Work with a partner. Write a short sentence, such as 'I love hot chocolate'. Now say this sentence to each other in as many different ways as possible to imply different meanings and emotions.

How many different ways could you manage? How does this compare with others in your group?

Verbal communication

From Activity 2, you will have discovered that it is not just the words that convey meaning, but the way that they are spoken.

Research study

Argyle, Alkema and Gilmour (1971)

Aim: To see if tone of voice has any effect when interpreting a verbal message.

Method: Different groups of participants listened to either friendly or hostile messages spoken in either friendly or hostile tones of voice. Therefore, some participants heard a hostile message spoken in a friendly tone of voice and others heard a friendly message spoken in a hostile tone of voice.

Results: When participants were asked to interpret the messages, it was found that tone of voice had about five times the effect of the verbal message itself.

Conclusion: Tone of voice is extremely important in how people interpret verbal messages.

Research study

Davitz and Davitz (1961)

Aim: To see the effect of paralinguistics on the assessment of emotion.

Method: Participants were asked to listen to tape recordings and to assess the speakers' emotions from the paralinguistic cues: tone of voice, emphasis and intonation.

Results: There was a very high level of accuracy in recognising these emotions: affection, amusement, disgust and fear.

Conclusion: Paralinguistics has great importance when judging emotion.

> **Did you know ??????**
>
> In trying to work out the total impact of a message, psychologists have suggested that 7 per cent is verbal (the words used), 38 per cent is vocal (tone of voice) and 55 per cent is non-verbal (body language).

> **Activity**
>
> 3 What do you think of the studies of verbal communication that have been described? Working with a partner, try to think of at least **two** criticisms (evaluations).

Evaluation

You may have said that these studies help us to understand how some people might have problems getting verbal information across to other people if their words seem to contradict the tone of voice that they are using. It may also suggest that they are not being entirely truthful.

It is also true that these studies were carried out in rather artificial conditions where participants were asked to concentrate on different aspects of the communication. In real life, people may not focus so much on these details and be more taken in by the actual words used.

> **Check your understanding**
>
> 1 Distinguish between verbal and non-verbal communication. *(3 marks)*
>
> 2 Explain what is meant by 'paralinguistics'. *(3 marks)*
>
> 3 Describe and evaluate **one** study in which verbal communication was investigated. *(6 marks)*

> **AQA Examiner's tip**
>
> When distinguishing between two terms, remember that examples can be helpful and could earn extra marks.

How do we use eye contact and facial expression?

1 Working with a partner, have a five-minute conversation about anything you like. While you are having that conversation, be aware of what their eyes are doing.

Activity

1 Now that you have done the Starter activity, work in a group of four and try to answer the following questions.

a Do you think you had a normal conversation during that activity? Why?

b You were asked to be aware of what their eyes were doing. Did that make a difference to the way the conversation went?

c For how much of the conversation did you look at your partner's face? How much did they look at you?

d Did you look at your partner's face more when you were speaking or listening?

e Did you make **eye contact** with your partner? If so, how long did it last?

The activity asked you to be aware of the other person's eyes, so you may have felt a bit uncomfortable or embarrassed having that short conversation. Eye movements in conversation usually happen automatically. We are almost unaware that they are happening and yet eye movements have very important functions. According to Argyle (1975), they help to make the conversation flow smoothly; they give feedback about how you are being received by the other person and they can help to express emotions.

Functions of eye contact

Research study

Kendon (1967)

Aim: To see how eye movements affect the flow of conversation.

Method: Pairs of participants were asked to get acquainted. Their conversations were secretly watched by observers through a one-way mirror system.

Results: As one person was about to speak, they looked away from the other person, briefly avoiding eye contact. Then they would give the other person's face a prolonged look when they were about to finish what they were saying. When the speaker gave the prolonged look, it seemed to indicate to the other person that they could begin to speak. If the prolonged look didn't happen, there was a pause in the conversation.

Conclusion: Eye movements signal turn taking in conversation.

Objectives

You will be able to:

understand the functions of eye contact

understand categories of facial expression

understand the link between facial expressions and hemispheres of the brain

describe and evaluate studies of eye contact and facial expression

understand practical implications of eye contact and facial expression.

Key terms

Eye contact: when two people in conversation are looking at each other's eyes at the same time.

Pupil dilation: when the pupils in the eyes expand to look large.

A *She gives a prolonged look. He looks away as he is about to speak*

Did you know ??????

When two people are having a conversation, they look at the other person twice as much when they are listening as when they are talking. Each look usually lasts three to seven seconds. Eye contact usually lasts one to three seconds.

Research studies

Argyle (1968)

Aim: To see how interrupting eye contact affects conversation.

Method: Pairs of participants were observed having conversations. In half the conversations, one of the participants wore dark glasses so that the other could not receive eye contact.

Results: When one of the participants wore dark glasses, there were more pauses and interruptions than when dark glasses were not worn.

Conclusion: Eye contact is important in ensuring the smooth flow of conversation.

Hess (1963)

Aim: To see the effect of **pupil dilation** on emotion.

Method: Participants were shown two nearly identical pictures of the same girl and asked which picture was more attractive. The only difference between the two pictures was that, in one of them, the girl's pupils were dilated, and in the other picture they were not.

Results: The majority of participants said that the picture of the girl with dilated pupils was more attractive. Strangely though, they could not say why they thought that.

Conclusion: Pupil dilation has an unconscious but powerful effect on emotion.

Activity

2   What do you think of the studies of eye contact that have been described? Working with a partner, try to think of at least **two** criticisms (evaluations).

Evaluation

Asking people to get acquainted and then observing them is a very artificial situation and participants may have behaved in a different way to normal (as you may have done in the Starter activity). However, studies of eye contact help us to understand what we can do to make conversations run more smoothly.

Studies of pupil dilation help us to understand why the use of eye makeup is so popular. It has the effect of making the eyes look darker and larger, which seems to be an important unconscious signal for attraction.

2   Without looking back, what is meant by 'pupil dilation'?

Now, try to think of **three** functions of eye contact.

3   Now that you know about studies of eye contact and pupil dilation, what practical implications can you think of for this knowledge? Working with a partner, try to think of at least **two** practical implications. Also try to think of benefits and drawbacks that go with this. Don't read on until you have attempted this activity.

Practical implications

Studies of eye movements in conversation help us to understand why we might feel uncomfortable talking to someone who either constantly looks at us or never looks at us at all. You are never quite sure when it is your turn to say something.

We have no control over pupil dilation. It is biologically programmed into us. A drawback of this could be that we cannot hide our emotions if we are attracted to someone (without wearing dark glasses).

Facial expression

Osgood (1966) found that the seven facial expressions that you attempted in Activity 4 are recognised in virtually all societies. This probably means that they are inherited. As humans, we have more muscles for moving our faces than any other animal. Our facial expressions can change very rapidly; some may last for just 0.2 of a second. All this is controlled by the two **hemispheres of the brain**.

Sackeim (1978)

Aim: To look at the relationship between facial expressions and the hemispheres of the brain.

Method: Pictures of people's faces showing different emotions were cut down the middle. New pictures were created with each half face and its mirror image. Then each pair of new faces was shown to participants. They were asked which picture they liked better.

Results: The majority of participants said they preferred the picture of the left half face and its reflection. When asked why, they said the person in the picture looked 'warmer'.

Conclusion: The left side of the face seems to express emotion much more than the right side.

Other research has shown that our emotions are contained in the right hemispheres of our brains. Sackeim's study makes sense, as the right hemisphere controls the left side of the body and vice versa. Therefore, we would expect emotion to show more on the left side of the face.

Hemispheres of the brain: the human brain is divided into two halves, called the left and right hemispheres.

4   Working in a group, write each of these words on seven separate pieces of paper: 'happy', 'surprised', 'angry', 'afraid', 'sad', 'interested' and 'disgusted'. Now put these pieces of paper into a container.

Get a member of your group to take one piece of paper from the container and act out the facial expression. Everyone else in the group should write down what they think the expression is. How many were correct?

Try this again with each of the other words. Were some expressions easier to guess than others?

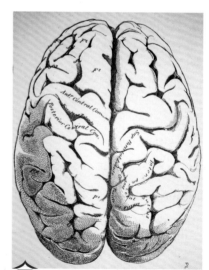

B   *The two hemispheres of the human brain viewed from above*

C *Happiness*

D *Surprise*

E *Anger*

F *Fear*

G *Sadness*

H *Interest*

I *Disgust*

Activity

5   What do you think of the studies of facial expression that have been described? Working with a partner, try to think of at least **two** criticisms (evaluations). Don't read on until you have attempted this activity.

Evaluation

Studies that involve still pictures are artificial. We don't usually stare at still pictures to judge people's emotions. Facial expressions in the real word change constantly when people are together. Also, we don't look at facial expression in isolation when we are with other people. Other aspects of their non-verbal behaviour can give more accurate cues to what they may be thinking, such as their posture or even style of dress.

Practical implications

If facial expression is inherited, this means that it happens instinctively and it is more likely to be truthful. Therefore, if someone is saying happy things with a sad facial expression, the chances are that person is feeling sad. It is easy to lie with words, but less easy with facial expression.

Sackeim's study also helps us to understand why we prefer certain picture profiles of ourselves rather than others. We prefer to show our warm side.

Activity

6   Now that you know about studies of facial expression, what **practical implications** can you think of for this knowledge? Working with a partner, try to think of at least **two** practical implications. Also try to think of benefits and drawbacks that go with this.

Key terms

Practical implications: suggestions about behaviour in the real world beyond the research study, based upon what psychologists have discovered.

Check your understanding

1   Decide whether each of the following statements is **true** or **false**:

a   Facial expressions are inherited. *(1 mark)*

b   Emotions are contained in the left hemisphere of the brain. *(1 mark)*

2   Outline **two** practical implications of studies of facial expressions. *(4 marks)*

Did you know ??????

Research has shown that women's facial expressions are more expressive than men's. Women are also more accurate than men in correctly interpreting the facial expressions of others.

How do we use body language?

1 Take two minutes to write down what you think would be a good definition for the term **body language**.

Activity

1 Ask every member of your group to either stand or sit in pairs and have a conversation with each other.

After about two minutes look around and notice what **postures** they have adopted.

How many are sitting or standing in a way that mirrors the other person's posture? How many are not?

Posture

People who are getting on well together tend to adopt each other's posture when they are having a conversation. This is known as **postural echo**.

Research study

McGinley (1975)

Aim: To see the effect of postural echo when having a conversation.

Method: A **confederate** of the experimenter approached individuals in a social setting and had conversations with them. In half of the meetings, the confederate echoed the posture of the person they were talking to. In the rest of the meetings, the confederate did not echo the posture of the other person. Afterwards, the experimenter approached the individuals and asked them what they thought of the confederate.

Results: When postural echo was used, the people questioned liked the confederate and thought that they got on well together. When postural echo was not used, the confederate was not liked as much and the conversation felt awkward.

Conclusion: Postural echo gives an unconscious message of friendliness.

Activity

2 Ask every member of your group to stand in pairs facing each other.

Now ask them to have a two-minute conversation with each other. For half of the conversation tell them to make sure their arms are folded across their chests. For the other half of the conversation, make sure their arms are not crossed.

Did the two types of posture make any difference to the way the conversations went? How did you feel talking to someone with their arms crossed?

Objectives

You will be able to:

recognise different types of body language

describe and evaluate studies of body language

understand practical implications of studies of body language.

Key terms

Body language: a general term to describe aspects of non-verbal communication.

Posture: the positioning of the body, often regarded as a non-verbal communication signal.

Postural echo: mirroring another person's body position.

Confederate: an actor or stooge who appears to be a genuine participant in the experiment but is actually working for the experimenter.

Closed posture: positioning the arms so that they are folded across the body and/or crossing the legs.

Open posture: positioning the arms so they are not folded across the body and not crossing the legs.

A *People who get on well together tend to reflect each other's posture*

Crossing your arms while you are in conversation is known as **closed posture**. Psychologists say that this could indicate rejection or disagreement. Having your arms uncrossed and relaxed is known as **open posture**. This may indicate approval or acceptance.

B   *Open posture: 'I am happy to hear your ideas'*

> ### McGinley, Lefevre and McGinley (1975)
>
> **Aim:** To see the effect of open and closed posture when having a conversation.
>
> **Method:** A confederate of the experimenter approached individuals in a social setting and had conversations with them. In half of the conversations the confederate adopted an open posture. In the other half, the confederate adopted a closed posture. Afterwards, the experimenter approached the individuals and asked them what they thought of the confederate.
>
> **Results:** When showing an open posture, the confederate was seen as friendly and attractive. When showing a closed posture, the confederate was seen as unfriendly and less attractive.
>
> **Conclusion:** The posture that someone adopts can make a difference to how much they are liked.

Research study

C   *Closed posture: 'I am not happy about what you are saying'*

Activity

3   What do you think of the studies of posture that have been described? Working with a partner, try to think of at least **two** criticisms (evaluations). Don't read on until you have attempted this activity.

Evaluation

You may have strong views about using confederates in studies such as these. The individuals who were approached did not realise that they were being used as participants in research. This is deception and could be regarded as unethical.

You may have realised that apart from open and closed posture there could be other factors causing the difference in results. For example, because of the experimental design used, personality differences between the people approached may have made the confederate more appealing to some than others.

Practical implications

These studies highlight how people in the real world may be using this information to their advantage. For example, counsellors might deliberately use postural echo to develop closer relationships with their clients. The implication for their clients is that they might divulge more about themselves to a counsellor who uses postural echo.

Also, salespeople might use open postures when talking to customers because it might help them to make a sale. An implication for the customer who does not know about these studies is that they might not realise how they are being manipulated.

⬯⬯ links

See Topic 5.4 for more information about ethical issues in psychological research.

See Topic 5.1 for more information about experimental design.

Activity

4   Now that you know about studies of posture, what practical implications can you think of for this knowledge? Working with a partner, try to think of at least **two** practical implications. Also try to think of benefits and drawbacks that go with this.

Did you know ??????

Psychologists have found a relationship between posture and status. A high-status person is likely to adopt a relaxed stance, often with hands in pockets. A low-status person generally has a more rigid posture.

2 Without looking back, explain **three** ways that posture might be used to communicate non-verbally.

D Peace

E OK?   **F** Call me?

Gestures

The gestures we make communicate additional information to people. Some gestures are deliberate to emphasise what we are saying or to affect the behaviour of another person. Other gestures are unconscious and sometimes we do not realise that we are giving away information, for example, by nervously tapping our fingers or even just raising an eyebrow.

Lynn and Mynier (1993)

Aim: To see the effect of gestures used by waiters and waitresses on the tipping behaviour of customers in a restaurant.

Method: While taking orders from seated customers, waiters and waitresses were instructed to either stand upright or squat down near the customer (squatting down makes more eye contact possible).

Results: When the waiters and waitresses squatted down, larger tips were received compared with when they took orders standing upright.

Conclusion: The gesture of squatting down near a seated customer to take an order will have a positive effect on tipping behaviour.

Touch

Touch is another non-verbal communication signal. It is a very powerful signal that can produce unconscious emotional reactions. There are huge cultural differences in the amount of touch that is permitted between individuals. British society seems to be more restricted than other Western societies in its use of touch when communicating.

G Touch: a very powerful social signal

5 Here is a chance to have some fun, but try not to be rude! Working with a partner, decide on five common **gestures** that are used to convey messages in our society.

With your teacher's permission, demonstrate these gestures to the rest of your group.

If other pairs in your group are doing this activity, how many different recognised gestures have you identified in total?

Gesture: a form of non-verbal communication in which information is conveyed by either deliberate or unconscious movement of parts of the body.

Touch: a form of non-verbal communication in which information is conveyed by physical contact between people.

The handshake as a gesture is quite a recent addition to British society. Until the 17th century, people would bow or curtsey instead. The handshake was only used to seal agreements.

Fisher, Rytting and Heslin (1976)

Aim: To see the effect of touch on people's attitudes.

Method: Female students in a library were handed books by the librarian. The librarian was a confederate of the experimenter. Half of the students were briefly touched on the hand by the librarian when the books were handed to them. The other students were not touched by the librarian.

Results: When questioned later, the students who were touched had a much more positive attitude towards the library and the librarian than those who were not touched. The interesting thing was that the students were not aware that they had been touched.

Conclusion: Touch can have an unconscious and positive effect on attitudes.

Research study

Did you know ???????

One experiment found that two-thirds of women agreed to dance with a man who touched their arm for a second while asking them for a dance. When the same man did not use touch, his success rate halved.

Evaluation

In the Lynn and Mynier study, there might have been other reasons for the difference in tips given. For example, the size of the bill usually affects the size of the tip. Also, whether the customer was served by someone of the same or the opposite sex might have been another factor. However, the study does show how knowledge of the effect of gestures can be used to people's advantage.

In the library study, the participants were all female. Therefore, we do not know if males would have been affected in the same way. You may also have questioned the ethics of that study because the females did not know until later that they were being used as participants in the experiment.

Activity

6   What do you think of the studies of gesture and touch that have been described? Working with a partner, try to think of at least **two** criticisms (evaluations).

Activity

7   Now that you know about studies of gesture and touch, what practical implications can you think of for this knowledge? Working with a partner, try to think of at least **two** practical implications. Also try to think of benefits and drawbacks that go with this. Don't read on until you have attempted this activity.

Going further

Working with a partner, design and carry out an investigation into body language. Then report your findings to your group.

Remember that a psychological investigation should start with a hypothesis.

Practical implications

One famous restaurant chain trains its waiters and waitresses to squat down when taking orders at tables. Unsuspecting customers probably see this as a friendly gesture, but studies such as the one conducted by Lynn and Mynier suggest that there could be other motives.

Studies of touch also show how attitudes in the real world might be manipulated by people who want to win favour.

∞ links

See Chapters 5 and 10 for more information about how to design and carry out an investigation.

Check your understanding

1   Distinguish between open posture and closed posture. *(3 marks)*

2   Explain **one** practical implication of studies of body language. *(3 marks)*

AQA Examiner's tip

Remember that for each mark available, you should try to add an additional piece of information to your answer.

2.4 How important is personal space?

Objectives

You will be able to:

understand factors that affect personal space

describe and evaluate studies of factors that affect personal space

understand practical implications of studies of factors that affect personal space.

Starter activity

1. a Stand as close to your neighbour as feels comfortable for you. Try doing this facing each other. How far apart are you standing?
   b Now do the same thing, side by side. How far apart are you now?
   c Now try it back to back and note the distance. Were there differences in how far apart you stood each time?

The distance that feels comfortable between you and the other person is known as your **personal space**. This distance varies depending on the circumstances you are in. After eye contact, personal space is perhaps the second most important non-verbal communication signal that we use.

Activity

1. Working with a partner, try to think of how being male or female might affect personal space. Do you think this might make a difference? If so, how?

Key terms

Personal space: the distance we keep between ourselves and other people in our everyday lives.

Sex differences: differences due to being either male or female; these could affect personal space between individuals.

Individual differences: factors that make one person not the same as another person, such as personality or age.

Sex differences

Research study

Argyle and Dean (1965)

Aim: To see if **sex differences** affect personal space.

Method: One at a time, participants were asked to sit and have a conversation with another person who was actually a confederate of the experimenter. Sometimes the confederate was the same sex as the participant and at other times the confederate was of the opposite sex. The confederate sat at different distances from the participant and continually looked into the participant's eyes.

Results: The participants tended to break eye contact with the confederate of the opposite sex at a greater distance apart than when the confederate was of the same sex. Argyle and Dean thought that this was the point at which personal space was being invaded.

Conclusion: We prefer to have a greater amount of personal space between ourselves and members of the opposite sex during normal conversation.

A *What factors might affect personal space here?*

Activity

2. What practical implications can you think of for knowledge of sex differences and personal space? Working with a partner, try to think of at least **two** practical implications. Also try to think of benefits and drawbacks of this. Don't read on until you have attempted this activity.

Practical implications

It could be that when a male is in conversation with a female, he might not be aware that he is standing too close for her comfort. For example, look at Photo **A**. Remember closed posture: do you think the woman wearing the blue blouse has folded her arms defensively because the man is standing too close to her?

Individual differences

> **Willis (1966)**
>
> **Aim:** To see if age has an effect on personal space.
>
> **Method:** Willis observed almost 800 individuals in different social situations.
>
> **Results:** Those he observed tended to stand closer to people their own age and further away from people who were either very much older or younger than themselves.
>
> **Conclusion:** Age difference affects how close people will stand to one another.

Research study

> **Williams (1971)**
>
> **Aim:** To see if personality has an effect on personal space.
>
> **Method:** College students were given personality tests to see if they were extrovert (outgoing and sociable) or introvert (quiet and reserved). They were then sent to an office one by one to receive their college grades from a tutor. The researchers noted where they chose to sit in the office when receiving their grades.
>
> **Results:** Introverts sat further away from the tutor than extroverts.
>
> **Conclusion:** Whether someone is extrovert or introvert will affect their use of personal space.

Research study

Activity

3　Working with a partner, try to think of how individual differences, such as your age, might affect personal space. Do you think this might make a difference? If so, how?

∞ links

See Topic 2.3 for information on closed posture.

B　*We tend to stand closer to people our own age*

Activity

4　What practical implications can you think of for this knowledge? Working with a partner, try to think of at least **two** practical implications. Also try to think of the benefits and drawbacks of this. Don't read on until you have attempted this activity.

Practical implications

People might think that, if a person older or younger than themselves stands further away, they are being unfriendly. However, the research shows that this is normal human behaviour. Another implication could be that, if we attempt to stand closer to a person older or younger than ourselves, it might cause them to feel uncomfortable. Also, if we are not sensitive to personality differences between ourselves and the people we talk to, we might not realise that we are causing them discomfort by standing too close to them.

Did you know ? ? ? ? ?

When a man passes a woman along a narrow corridor, he usually turns his body towards her as he passes, whereas she will usually turn her body away from his. Is this use of personal space learned or instinctive?

Starter activity

2   Without looking back, try to recall how sex differences and individual differences might affect personal space.

Activity

5   Working with a partner, think about how **cultural norms** might affect personal space. Would you expect to see differences between different cultures? If so, what might they be?

Cultural norms

Research study

Summer (1969)

Aim: To see if there are cultural differences in the use of personal space.

Method: Summer observed groups of white English people and groups of Arab people in conversation.

Results: The comfortable conversation distance for the white English people was 1–1.5 m, whereas the comfortable conversation distance for the Arab people was much less than that.

Conclusion: The use of personal space in normal conversation varies with culture.

Other research has shown that, when in conversation, people in Mediterranean cultures usually have a smaller amount of personal space between them than people in North European and American cultures.

Practical implications

This study could help us to understand why people in Arab countries regard Europeans and Americans as unfriendly and untrustworthy: it is because they tend to stand back during conversations. It also helps to explain why Mediterranean men are seen as romantic by British girls: they tend to stand closer than most British males.

Status

Research study

Zahn (1991)

Aim: To see if status has an effect on personal space.

Method: Zahn observed people of equal status approaching each other to have a conversation. He also observed people of unequal status approaching each other.

Results: Zahn found that people of lower status did not approach higher-status people with the same degree of closeness as those of equal status.

Conclusion: The use of personal space varies with differences in status when approaching other people.

Activity

6   What practical implications can you think of for this knowledge? Working with a partner, try to think of at least two practical implications. Also try to think of the benefits and drawbacks of this.

C   *Personal space during conversations tends to be less in Arab cultures*

Activity

7   Working with a partner, try to think of how **status** might affect personal space. Would you expect to see differences? If so, what might they be?

1 Try this on your own. When you are sitting at a meal table with someone, subtly move the salt towards them so they don't notice. If the salt enters their intimate zone, they will probably move it away. If it doesn't work with the salt alone, try moving other things too! This roughly shows the border of their intimate zone.

Also, when you are standing with someone in conversation, subtly try moving gradually towards them. They will probably back away to keep you somewhere in their personal zone. If you do this cleverly you can get them to walk backwards around the room you are in!

D *Status affects how close we stand to someone*

Activity

8 Now that you have read the study of status and personal space, what practical implications can you think of for this knowledge? Working with a partner, try to think of at least **two** practical implications. Also try to think of the benefits and drawbacks of this. Don't read on until you have attempted this activity.

Practical implications

This study might imply that it feels more threatening to approach someone of higher status and we show our anxiety by keeping our distance. It also implies that we feel more comfortable approaching people of equal status.

Activity

9 What do you think of the studies of factors that affect personal space that have been described? Working with a partner, try to think of at least **four** criticisms (evaluations). Don't read on until you have attempted this activity.

Evaluation

Although these factors are useful in giving a general view of how personal space is used, they can also be misleading. This is because these factors do not operate in isolation from other aspects of non-verbal communication. For example, the other person's facial expression could affect our use of personal space. How close would you stand to someone of equal status who looks angry? Apart from that, when we are with people, we probably use a number of different distances depending on what is happening at the time and how much physical space there is available. Other factors, such as how much we like the other person or whether we have an outgoing or reserved personality, also come into play.

Did you know ??????

Psychologists have found that our personal space has four zones: an intimate zone (less than 0.5 m) into which we allow only very close friends; a personal zone (0.5–1.2 m) for casual acquaintances; a social zone (1.2–3.6 m) for people we don't know very well; and a public zone (over 3.6 m) for more formal occasions such as speaking to an audience.

Going further

2 Working with a partner, design a visual aid to non-verbal communication. This could be a poster using images that could be displayed in your classroom or a spider diagram that incorporates all of the key features of this topic.

Check your understanding

1 Identify **three** factors that affect personal space. *(3 marks)*

2 Describe and evaluate **one** study in which a factor affecting personal space was investigated. *(6 marks)*

3 Using your knowledge of psychology, explain **one** practical implication of studies of factors affecting personal space. *(3 marks)*

AQA Examiner's tip

Remember that evaluations are not just personal opinions. They must be backed up with relevant knowledge of psychology.

3 Development of personality

3.1 What is personality?

Objectives

You will be able to:

define personality

define temperament

describe the studies of temperament carried out by Thomas, Buss and Plomin, and Kagan

evaluate the studies of temperament carried out by Thomas, Buss and Plomin, and Kagan.

Starter activity

1. Describe the personalities of the people in Photos **A**, **B**, **C** and **D**.

A Amy Winehouse

B Wayne Rooney

C Simon Cowell

D Victoria Beckham

Defining personality and temperament

Although we are able to describe the **personality** of the people around us, defining what we mean by 'personality' is more difficult.

Personality is made up of the thoughts, feelings and behaviours that make a person unique. It therefore comes from within the individual and remains reasonably constant. This means that the person is the same in different situations. Personality can develop over the years as a result of experience.

Temperament refers to the inherited aspects of personality. Therefore, it describes the way in which the individual responds to the environment. This stays constant throughout life.

Understanding temperament can be important in helping people to recognise which situations they may find difficult. Although they cannot change their temperament, they can find ways of dealing with these situations. For example, if someone is easily distracted they might learn to remove all distractions before starting an important task.

Key terms

Personality: the thoughts, feelings and behaviours that make an individual unique.

Temperament: the genetic component of personality.

Longitudinal study: a study carried out to show how behaviour changes over time.

Going further

1. Interview someone who knew you as a baby.

a. Ask them:
   - Did I fall asleep at the same time every night?
   - Did I wake up at the same time every morning?
   - Did I want to be fed at the same times everyday?
   - Did I smile often?
   - How did I react to change?

b. Are you still the same now?

c. Have you found ways of dealing with your sleep patterns?

d. Have you found ways of dealing with change?

■ Studies of temperament

Thomas, Chess and Birch (1977)

Aim: To discover whether ways of responding to the environment remain stable throughout life.

Method: They studied 133 children from infancy to early adulthood. The children's behaviour was observed and their parents were interviewed. The parents were asked about the child's routine and its reactions to change.

Results: They found that the children fell into three types: 'easy', 'difficult' or 'slow to warm up'. The 'easy' children were happy, flexible and regular. The 'difficult' children were demanding, inflexible and cried a lot. The children that were 'slow to warm up' did not respond well to change or new experiences to begin with, but once they had adapted they were usually happy.

Conclusion: These ways of responding to the environment stayed with the children as they developed. Thomas, Chess and Birch therefore concluded that temperament is innate.

E *Easy*

Activity

1 What do you think of Thomas, Chess and Birch's study? Evaluate it with a partner:

a This was a longitudinal study. Outline one advantage and one disadvantage of this.

b All the children were from middle-class families. What is the drawback of choosing all the participants from one social class?

c The parents were interviewed for this study. Outline one drawback of asking parents about their children.

F *Difficult*

Evaluation

■ This is one of the few **longitudinal studies** of temperament allowing the researchers to support the view that temperament is innate. This is because if the children still show the same reactions to situations as they get older, this would suggest it is an inborn response. The drawback of longitudinal studies, however, is that some participants could drop out partway through, which could affect the results.

■ The children were from middle-class families living in New York. This means the results cannot be generalised to other social classes.

■ The parents may have been biased in the answers they gave in the interviews. They may have given answers that they thought showed their children in the best possible way.

G *Slow to warm up*

Did you know ??????

The ancient Greeks were the first people to identify different temperaments.

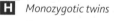

Starter activity

Starter activity

2 Your teacher will give you a description of the Thomas, Chess and Birch study, but the sentences will all be in the wrong order. Rearrange them so that you have got an accurate description of this study.

Key terms

Monozygotic twins: twins developed from one fertilised egg.

Dizygotic twins: twins developed from two separately fertilised eggs.

■ Other studies into temperament

Research study

Buss and Plomin (1984)

Aim: To test the idea that temperament is innate.

Method: They studied 228 pairs of **monozygotic twins** and 172 pairs of **dizygotic twins**. They rated the temperament of the twins when they were five years old. They looked at three dimensions of behaviour:

- emotionality – how strong the child's emotional response was
- activity – how energetic the child was
- sociability – how much the child wanted to be with other people.

They then compared the scores for each pair of twins.

Results: There was a closer correlation between the scores of the monozygotic twins than between the scores of the dizygotic twins.

Conclusion: Temperament has a genetic basis.

H *Monozygotic twins*

I *Dizygotic twins*

Activity

2 Outline **two** drawbacks of carrying out research using twins and then check your answers with the points below.

Evaluation

- This study supports the view that temperament is innate. This is because the monozygotic twins, who are genetically identical, were more similar in emotionality, activity and sociability than the dizygotic twins, who are only as genetically similar as any other siblings.

- Monozygotic twins are treated in very similar ways. The correlation between their scores could therefore be explained by their environment rather than by their genes.

- Research carried out on twins cannot be generalised to the whole population because not everyone is a twin.

Kagan and Snidman (1991)

Aim: To investigate whether temperament is due to biological differences.

Method: Kagan and Snidman studied the reactions of four-month-old babies to new situations. For the first minute the baby was placed in a seat with the caregiver sitting nearby. For the next three minutes the caregiver moved out of the baby's view while the baby was shown different toys by the researcher.

Results: Twenty per cent of the babies showed distress by crying, vigorous movement of the arms and legs and arching of the back. They were classed as high reactive. Forty per cent of the babies showed little movement or emotion. They were classed as low reactive. The remaining infants fell somewhere between the two.

In a follow-up study, 11 years later, Kagan and Snidman found there was still a difference in the way the two groups reacted to new situations; the high reactives were shy while the low reactives were calm.

Conclusion: Kagan and Snidman concluded that these two temperaments are due to inherited differences in the way the brain responds.

Activity

3 What do you think of Kagan and Snidman's study? Evaluate it with a partner:

a Kagan and Snidman studied 500 babies. What is the advantage of having a large sample?

b The study was carried out in an experimental setting. Outline **one** advantage and **one** disadvantage of carrying out research in an experimental setting.

c The reactions of the babies were observed and recorded. What is the disadvantage of observing behaviour?

Evaluation

- Kagan and Snidman used a large sample, which means it is easier to generalise their results to the whole population.

- The research took place in an experimental setting. This is a controlled environment that would not have been familiar to the children taking part in the study. Therefore they may have behaved differently from usual because they were in a strange place.

- Behaviour was observed and recorded. The researchers may have missed some important behaviours or recorded them inaccurately. This would affect the results.

∞ links

See Topic 10.2 for more about observation studies.

Going further

2 Identify your temperament by going to **www.ptypes.com/ temperament_test.html**

AQA Examiner's tip

The specification includes studies of temperament by:

- Thomas, Chess and Birch
- Buss and Plomin
- Kagan and Snidman.

It is therefore important that you learn all three. You could be asked, for example, to describe a study carried out by Buss and Plomin to investigate temperament.

Check your understanding

1 Define what is meant by 'personality'. *(2 marks)*

2 Define what is meant by 'temperament'. *(2 marks)*

3 Describe **one** study of temperament. In your answer include the reason the study was carried out, the method used, the results obtained and the conclusion drawn. *(4 marks)*

4 Evaluate the study you have described in Question 3. *(3 marks)*

3.2 How is personality measured?

Starter activity

1 Copy and complete the following definition of personality:

The t_____, f_____ and b_____ that make a person u_____.

Eysenck's type theory of personality

Eysenck believed that there are different personality types. His theory is therefore described as a **type theory**. For each personality type there are associated traits. The personality types he identified include **extroversion**, **introversion** and **neuroticism**. Extroverts look to other people and the outside world for entertainment while introverts are content with their own thoughts and ideas.

Activity

1 Copy this table. Then, under each of the following personality types, write traits that you think go with each type. One example of each type has been done for you.

Extrovert	Introvert	Neurotic
sociable	quiet	anxious

Extroverts, introverts and neurotics have been described in the following way.

Objectives

You will be able to:

describe and evaluate Eysenck's type theory of personality

define 'extroversion', 'introversion' and 'neuroticism'

describe the EPI and EPQ personality scales.

Key terms

Type theory: personality types are thought to be inherited. They can be described using related traits.

Extroversion: a personality type that describes people who look to the outside world for entertainment.

Introversion: a personality type that describes people who are content with their own company.

Neuroticism: a personality type that describes people who are highly emotional and show a quick, intense reaction to fear.

A *Extroverts are sociable, lively and easy-going. They seem to need to have other people around. They have many friends and enjoy parties and practical jokes*

B *Introverts like to spend time alone. They have a small number of very close friends. They are usually serious, organised and like routine*

C *Neurotics are anxious, irritable, tense, shy and moody. They are lacking in confidence and self-esteem*

Eysenck believed that these different personality types were caused by the type of nervous system that the individual inherits. For example, in neurotics, the nervous system reacts quickly and strongly to stress.

Research study

Eysenck (1947)

Aim: To investigate the personality of 700 servicemen.

Method: Each soldier completed a questionnaire. Eysenck analysed the results using a statistical technique known as factor analysis.

Results: He identified two dimensions of personality: extroversion–introversion and neuroticism–stability.

Conclusion: Everyone can be placed along these two dimensions of personality. Most people lie in the middle of the scale.

Evaluation

- His original research used a limited sample to test his ideas (the research was only carried out on servicemen). Since then, however, his findings have been supported by further research carried out on thousands of people.
- He only described a limited number of personality types.
- He used questionnaires to test personality. The answers people gave could have been based on their mood at the time.
- He believed that personality is genetic. This does not consider the idea that personality can change as a result of experience.

Activity

2   What do you think of Eysenck's theory? Evaluate this theory with a partner:

a   What was the drawback of only studying servicemen?

b   What was the drawback of asking the servicemen to complete questionnaires about themselves?

c   What is the drawback of stating that personality is inherited?

Did you know ??????

Both of Eysenck's parents were actors and he appeared in a film at the age of three.

Personality scales

Eysenck developed **personality scales** in order to measure personality types.

The Eysenck Personality Inventory (EPI)

This scale is used to measure extroversion–introversion and neuroticism–stability. It is made up of a series of yes/no questions. The answers given can be used to identify an individual's personality. The two dimensions are not related so the individual can be identified as a neurotic extrovert, a neurotic introvert, a stable extrovert or a stable introvert.

The Eysenck Personality Questionnaire (EPQ)

This scale is also used to measure extroversion, introversion and neuroticism. A further dimension added to this scale is known as **psychoticism**. Most people score low on this dimension, but those with a high score are hostile, aggressive, insensitive, cruel and lacking in feelings. Again the three dimensions are not linked. This means that the individual is given a separate score for extroversion, neuroticism and psychoticism.

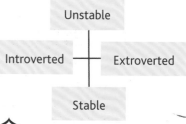

D Two personality dimensions

E Exhibiting some traits of psychoticism

Activity

3 Identify **two** traits that each of the following individuals might have:

a a neurotic extrovert

b a neurotic introvert.

stable extrovert sociable, outgoing, talkative, responsive, easy-going, lively, carefree	**stable introvert** calm, even-tempered, reliable, controlled, peaceful, thoughtful, careful
unstable extrovert touchy, restless, aggressive excitable, changeable, impulsive, optimistic	**unstable introvert** moody, anxious, pessimistic, reserved, unsociable, quiet

 Traits associated with Eysenck's personality types

Going further

Carry out Eysenck's Personality Questionnaire on the internet. Try the test on this website: www.similarminds.com/eysenck.html

Do you agree with the results?

Check your understanding

1 Lisa does not like being alone. She is sociable, makes friends easily and loves going to parties. Identify which personality type Lisa has. *(1 mark)*   S E

2 Luke is easily frightened and upset. He worries about things that have happened or are going to happen. Identify which personality type Luke has. *(1 mark)*   U I

3 Evaluate Eysenck's type theory of personality. *(3 marks)*

4 Describe the EPQ personality scale. *(3 marks)*

3.3　What is Antisocial Personality Disorder?

Starter activity

Look at the pictures in **A**. Which ones do you think are showing antisocial behaviour?

Identify other antisocial behaviours.

Discuss your ideas with the rest of your group.

Objectives

You will be able to:

define what is meant by Antisocial Personality Disorder

identify at least three characteristics of Antisocial Personality Disorder.

A

People with **Antisocial Personality Disorder (APD)** do not have poor social skills. APD is a condition where individuals ignore the rights of others and do not use socially acceptable behaviour.

They do not abide by the law. They lie, steal and can be aggressive. They find it difficult to hold down a job and meet their responsibilities as a spouse or parent. They can have difficulty making or keeping friends, but they can also be witty and charming. APD affects 3 per cent of males and 1 per cent of females. About 75 per cent of the prison population suffer from this disorder.

Key terms

Antisocial Personality Disorder (APD): a condition in which the individual does not use socially acceptable behaviour or consider the rights of others.

Did you know　?????

People with APD used to be known as psychopaths or, more recently, as sociopaths.

Helen

Helen is 30 years old. When she was a teenager she was often in trouble both at school and at home. As an adult she has been unable to hold down a job. She has little empathy for the feelings of others and often steals from her mother. She has difficulty making friendships but is able to manipulate others into getting want she wants. She was arrested for shoplifting but managed to persuade the police officer that she had not been stealing the item but had forgotten to pay for it.

Activity

1   Working in pairs, list the reasons why Helen could be diagnosed with APD.

■ Characteristics of APD

The Diagnostic and Statistical Manual of Mental Disorders, Fourth Edition – Text Revision (American Psychiatric Association, 2000), better known as the **DSM-IV TR** (2000), covers all the mental health disorders for both children and adults. It includes information about each disorder including the age at which it starts, the criteria used for diagnosis and the causes.

APD cannot be diagnosed until the individual is at least 18 years old, but they will have been showing this pattern of behaviour from the age of 15.

To be diagnosed with APD the individual will show three or more of the following characteristics:

- not following the norms and laws of society
- being deceitful by lying, conning others and using aliases
- being impulsive and not planning ahead
- being irritable and aggressive, often involved in physical fights or assaults
- being careless about their own safety or the safety of others
- being irresponsible, failing to hold down a job or pay back money owed to others
- lacking remorse by being indifferent to, or finding reasons for, hurting, mistreating or stealing from others.

These symptoms tend to be at their worst when the individual is in their teens or early twenties but get better with age.

Key terms

DSM-IV TR: lists different mental disorders and the criteria for diagnosing them.

AQA *Examiner's tip*

You will need to remember three of these characteristics for the exam.

Going further

1   Use the internet to research the personality of a known criminal.

a   Produce a wanted poster for this individual, which describes their personality.

b   Working in groups, look at the wanted posters you have made.

- ■ Identify which of the criminals you have described have APD.

- ■ Discuss your ideas with the rest of your group.

Activity

2   Reread the case study of Helen. She has symptoms that fit the DSM-IV diagnosis of APD. Outline **three** characteristics of the DSM-IV diagnosis shown by Helen.

Check your understanding

1   Define APD. *(2 marks)*

2   Outline **two** characteristics of APD. *(4 marks)*

Starter activity

1 Do you think serial killers are born with Antisocial Personality Disorder (APD) or do you think they develop this condition as a result of their upbringing? Write down your reasons and discuss them with the rest of your group.

Biological causes of APD

Some researchers believe that brain abnormalities are the main cause of APD. The amygdala and the prefrontal cortex are the two areas of the brain that have been associated with APD.

Background

The **amygdala** is located in the limbic system and is in the temporal lobe of the brain. It is involved in memory and emotion, particularly fear.

The outer layer of the brain is known as the cerebral cortex or **grey matter**. Grey matter includes regions of the brain involved in muscle control, sensory perceptions such as seeing and hearing, memory, emotions and speech.

The **prefrontal cortex** is located in the frontal lobe of the brain. It is involved in expressing personality and appropriate social behaviour.

Objectives

You will be able to:

describe the biological causes of Antisocial Personality Disorder

describe and evaluate a study by Raine of the biological causes of Antisocial Personality Disorder

describe the situational causes of Antisocial Personality Disorder

describe and evaluate studies by Farrington and by Elander of the situational causes of Antisocial Personality Disorder.

Key terms

Amygdala: part of the brain involved in emotion.

Grey matter (cerebral cortex): the outer layer of the brain.

Prefrontal cortex: the very front of the brain. It is involved in social and moral behaviour and controls aggression.

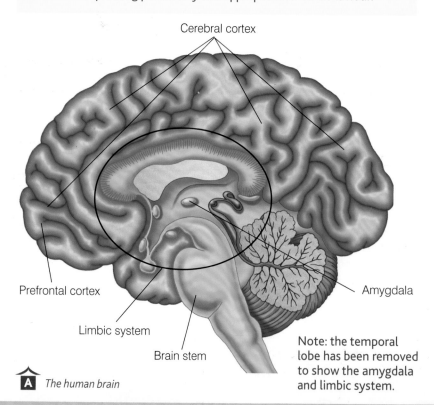

Cerebral cortex

Prefrontal cortex

Limbic system

Brain stem

Amygdala

Note: the temporal lobe has been removed to show the amygdala and limbic system.

A *The human brain*

The amygdala is responsible for learning from the negative consequences of our actions. It also responds to fearful and sad facial expressions in others. We therefore learn to avoid activities that we can see cause distress to others.

The amygdala is affected in people with APD. As a result, they do not learn to avoid behaviour that harms other people. This is because they are not affected by the distress shown by their victims.

Reduction in the grey matter in the prefrontal cortex of the brain has also been associated with APD. The prefrontal cortex is the area of the brain that enables people to learn social and moral behaviour and to feel guilt. As people with APD have reduced grey matter in this area, they are less likely to behave morally or to feel remorse for wrongdoing.

Did you know ??????

The amygdala gets its name from its shape – like an almond.

Activity

1 Work in pairs. Blow up a balloon and draw a face and ears on it. Now write on it where the amygdala and prefrontal cortex are.

Raine *et al.* (2000)

Aim: To support the theory that abnormalities in the prefrontal cortex cause APD.

Method: Magnetic resonance imaging (MRI) was used to study 21 men with APD and a control group of 34 healthy men. The subjects were all volunteers.

Results: The APD group had an 11 per cent reduction in prefrontal grey matter compared with the control group.

Conclusion: APD is caused by a reduction in the brain's grey matter.

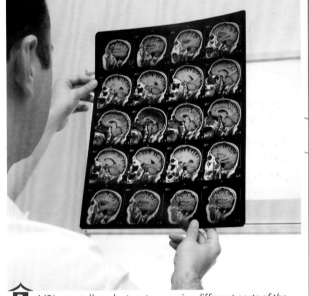

B *MRI scans allow doctors to examine different parts of the brain*

Research study

Activity

2 What do you think of this study? Working with a partner, try to think of at least **two** criticisms (evaluations). Don't read on until you have attempted this activity.

AQA Examiner's tip

When describing a study, write it under the headings 'Aim', 'Method', 'Results' and 'Conclusion'. This will help you to structure your answer.

Evaluation

- This study supports the biological explanation that APD is caused by an abnormality in the brain.
- Raine and his colleagues only studied males so their findings may not relate to women with APD.
- His participants were volunteers, so may not have been representative of all people with APD.
- Behaviours linked to one brain area often result from a deficit elsewhere in the brain. The cause of APD may therefore be more complex than this study suggests.

Starter activity

2   Draw a larger version of this shape in your notes. In each section, write something you have learnt about APD.

Situational causes of APD

APD may be caused by the situation that someone is brought up in. Therefore, some factors that lead to APD have their roots in childhood and include:

- **socioeconomic factors** including low family income and poor housing
- quality of life at home including poor parenting
- educational factors including low school achievement and leaving school at an early age.

Studies of the situational causes of APD

Research study

Farrington (1995)

Aim: To investigate the development of offending and antisocial behaviour in males studied from childhood to the age of 50.

Method: The researchers carried out a **longitudinal study** of the development of antisocial and offending behaviour in 411 males. They all lived in a deprived, inner-city area of London. They were first studied at the age of eight and were followed up until the age of 50. Their parents and teachers were also interviewed. Searches were carried out at the Criminal Records Office to discover if they, or members of their family, had been convicted of a crime.

Results: Forty-one per cent of the males were convicted of at least one offence between the ages of 10 and 50. The most important risk factors for offending were criminal behaviour in the family, low school achievement, poverty and poor parenting.

Conclusion: Situational factors lead to the development of antisocial behaviour.

C   *Do situational factors lead to antisocial behaviour?*

Activity

3   Work in pairs to identify the research method used in this study. Outline **one** limitation of this method of research. Don't read on until you have attempted this activity.

Evaluation

- This study was not a controlled experiment. Therefore, factors that were not considered could have affected the offending behaviour of the males studied. For example, biological factors were not investigated.
- The researchers in this study interviewed the males, their parents and teachers. When people are taking part in surveys they can give socially desirable answers.

Did you know ??????

Intervention programmes such as On Track have been designed to work with children as a way of reducing the likelihood of their developing antisocial behaviour as adults.

⊂⊃links

See Topic 10.1 for more about people giving the answers they think the researchers are looking for.

Elander et al. (2000a)

Aim: To investigate the childhood risk factors that can be used to predict antisocial behaviour in adulthood.

Method: Researchers investigated 225 twins who were diagnosed with childhood disorders and interviewed them 10–25 years later.

Results: Elander et al. found that childhood hyperactivity, conduct disorders, low IQ and reading problems were strong predictors of APD and criminality in adult life.

Conclusions: Disruptive behaviour in childhood can be used to predict APD in adulthood.

Evaluation

- This study supports the view that childhood risk factors make some people more likely to develop APD than others.
- This study looked at twins. Therefore, genetics, rather than situational factors, may have affected their behaviour.
- The participants were asked to describe experiences from their childhood, which they may have remembered wrongly.

Practical implications

Research into APD has implications for the prevention and treatment of this disorder:

- As researchers cannot decide on the cause of APD, it is difficult to know how to prevent and treat it.
- If APD has a biological cause then it cannot be prevented.
- Psychologists who believe APD has a biological cause have attempted to treat it using medication, but research has found this to be ineffective.
- If APD has a situational cause, then reducing childhood problems should lower the risk of APD developing.
- Identifying risk factors for APD can lead to some groups being overlooked. Children who have had a stable childhood can also develop APD.
- APD is one of the most difficult disorders to treat. The characteristics of this disorder can make patients difficult to work with. For example, they don't believe they need to change, or they lie about their behaviour and describe their offences as less serious than they were.

Check your understanding

1 Describe **one** study to support the biological explanation of APD. In your answer, include the reason the study was carried out, the method used, the results obtained and the conclusion drawn. (*4 marks*)

2 Outline the situational explanation of APD. (*2 marks*)

3 Outline **one** implication of research into APD. (*2 marks*)

Activities

4 a Explain one drawback to studying twins.

b Explain one difficulty with asking adults to recall events that happened in their childhood.

5 Your teacher will give you descriptions from the media of crimes that have been committed. Identify those where the person committing the crime may have APD. Does the news item suggest a possible reason for the crime? Choose one example and present your findings to the group.

6 Do the following to help you to revise this topic:

a Create revision cards of the key points.

b Draw a spider diagram to show how the points link together.

c Make a news bulletin of the key points.

Going further

1 Using the Internet, research the intervention programme On Track. Describe your findings to your group.

2 Play 'personality dominoes' on the AQA website: www.aqa.org.uk

4.1   What is stereotyping?

Starter activity

1   Divide a piece of paper into four sections. In each section, draw a quick sketch of a bus driver, nurse, scientist and chef. (If you are not very good at drawing, write down a list of words that you associate with each person.) Once you have finished, compare your sketches/words with your partner's and then the rest of your group. What similarities and differences are there between your pictures? What common **stereotypes** are there about these professions?

People tend to have stereotypes for different professions, cultures, ages, ethnicities, physical shapes and dress. Some commonly held stereotypes include elderly people walk with a stick; men are unemotional; *Guardian* readers are intelligent; a teenager in a hoody is up to no good.

By stereotyping, we make a snap judgement of someone and assign them to a category. For example, there has been a lot of bad press about teenagers in hoodies. If we come across a teenager in a hoody in the street, we are likely to be wary of them. This is because our stereotype of them is that they are all likely to cause trouble or to harm others.

Most stereotypes tend to give negative impressions, but they can also be positive. For example, overweight people are often seen as jolly, and black people are expected to be good athletes.

Objectives

You will be able to:

define stereotyping

understand how stereotyping can lead to positive and negative evaluations.

Key terms

Stereotype: an oversimplified, generalised set of ideas that we have about others, for example, secondary head teachers are strict, intimidating, scary and male.

A   *Some commonly held stereotypes*

Activity

1   Copy this table. Then select three characteristics from the box in the margin, which in your opinion best describe people of each nationality. List the characteristics under each heading. Characteristics can be used more than once.

Irish people	English people	German people	American people	Japanese people	Italian people

Compare your table with those of the rest of your group. What are the common stereotypes for each of the listed nationalities? Why do we have these stereotypes? Where do they come from? What problems could they cause?

Eat lots of pasta

Eat lots of fish

Have large cars and houses

Are jolly

Are friendly

Are grumpy

Are generous

Have blonde hair

Have dark hair

Watch football

Are miserable

Dress scruffily

Do well in business

Are intelligent

Are strict

Are hard working

Drink Guinness

Wear suits

Eat a lot

Drink a lot

Are short

Watch baseball

Have blue eyes

Dress smartly

Research into stereotyping

Research study

Williams and Best (1994)

Aim: To investigate the extent of sex stereotyping across 30 different countries.

Method: Participants were given over 300 characteristics and asked to state whether the characteristics were more likely to be associated with men, women or both sexes.

Results: They found that across the 30 countries the same characteristics tended to be associated with males and females. Females were described as 'understanding', 'emotional' and 'warm'. Males were described as 'reckless', 'hard-headed' and 'determined'.

Conclusion: The findings of this cross-cultural study suggest that there are commonly held stereotypes of males and females.

Psychologists have pointed out the negative consequences for females from sex role stereotyping. In children's programmes, books and films, females tended to be portrayed as the weaker sex. They were shown as dependent and unintelligent, while males were shown as being strong and dominant. However, over recent years, this has changed and males and females are now portrayed more equally.

Research study

Rubin *et al.* (1977)

Aim: To find out if new parents stereotype their babies.

Method: Parents were asked to describe their new babies within 24 hours of the baby being born.

Results: They found that parents of baby boys described their babies as being alert and strong, whereas parents of baby girls described their babies as soft and delicate.

Conclusion: Parents stereotype their children from a very early stage despite no stereotypical behaviour being shown. For a lot of parents who know the sex of their baby prior to birth, this stereotyping behaviour starts before the baby is born by painting a room pink for a girl or blue for a boy.

AQA *Examiner's tip*

Try to learn the definition of a 'stereotype'. In order to gain full marks for a 'define the term' question in the exam, you will need to give a precise definition of the term. For each mark that is available, a new point must be added or an example used.

B   *Newborn baby*

Going further

1   Ask some friends to give the first four words that come to mind when you present them with the following social groupings: people with blonde hair; people who are obese; male homosexuals; and unemployed people (or any groups of your choice). Record each of your friends' responses for the social groupings given. When you have done this, identify the similarities for each social group. What does this tell you about commonly held stereotypes?

Activity

2   Find a photo of a baby dressed in neutral colours. Make a list of 12 words that could describe a baby ('soft', 'alert', 'delicate', 'pretty', and so on). Have an equal number of masculine and feminine words. Show your list of words and the photo to about 10 people. For half of your participants, give them the following instruction: 'Look at the picture of the baby boy; choose two words from the list that you think best describe him'. For the other half of your participants, change the words 'boy' to 'girl' **and 'him' to 'her'**.

Did you find any differences between the way the baby was described depending on whether your participants believed it was a boy or a girl?

Starter activity

2 In pairs, list five groups of people you may have stereotypes for. Then for each group of people, list at least four characteristics you believe they may have. Now, go back through your list of characteristics and put a '+' sign next to the positive ones and a '−' sign next to the negative ones. Are there more positive or negative characteristics? Why do you think this is the case?

Practical implications of research into stereotyping

Activity

3 In pairs, or small groups, list as many children's programmes, films and books you can remember as a child. When you have done this, draw a table with three columns headed: 'Aimed at boys', 'Aimed at girls', 'Aimed at both'. Go back through your list and put each programme/film/book in one of the columns. What do you notice? Now for each category, make a few notes on the messages that the media is giving to children. What do you think children learn from these programmes? What changes have there been to children's media in recent years?

AQA Examiner's tip

It is important to learn what is meant by **practical implications**. In the exam you are very likely to be asked to give the practical implications of a theory at least once. 'Practical implications' means 'if this research is true, what does it suggest about behaviour in real life'.

Activity

4 Look at the four pictures in **C**. Explain why each picture goes against common stereotypes.

C Contrary to common stereotypes

There is an increased awareness that children do observe and imitate those around them, particularly **role models** from the media. This has led to a change in the way characters in children's programmes are portrayed. This is to prevent children from growing up believing that all females want to stay at home looking after children and are not capable of doing manual jobs. It is getting more popular nowadays for the father to stay at home and look after the children while the mother goes out to work. This would have been unheard of 50 years ago. A reduction in stereotypical views enables males to pursue careers previously only believed to have been suitable for females, such as childminders and nurses. The same goes for women in that they are pursuing careers that previously have been believed to be suitable for men only, such as mechanics and fire fighters.

■ Are stereotypes a good thing?

There are advantages and disadvantages to holding stereotypes. They can be very useful at times, but they can also be very detrimental.

Advantages of stereotyping include the following:

- They are helpful when we need to make snap judgements, when we don't have time to form a full impression of everyone we meet.
- They enable us to remember information about other people.
- They enable us to respond appropriately when we meet new people for the first time.
- They enable us to fit in with our own group and feel a sense of belonging.

Disadvantages of stereotyping include the following:

- They can stop us seeing the real person when we meet someone for the first time.
- Most stereotypes do promote harmful images.
- We can make mistakes about people when meeting them for the first time.
- Once learnt by children, they may be difficult to overcome.

Check your understanding

1 What is meant by the term 'stereotyping'? *(2 marks)*

2 Give an example of a group of people we may stereotype. List **two** characteristics of this group. *(2 marks)*

3 Outline **one** advantage and **one** disadvantage of stereotyping. *(4 marks)*

4 Explain **one** practical implication of the research on stereotyping. *(3 marks)*

⚭ links

See pages 128–9 of Topic 8.3 for more about the role the media plays in gender development.

Did you know ??????

Stereotyping is not always a negative thing to do. There are many advantages to stereotyping as well as the disadvantages. Most people do only see it as a negative though.

Going further

2 Make a list of about 15 traits (masculine, feminine and neutral such as hitting, kicking, helping, looking after children, fixing things, emotional, kind). Watch a few children's programmes that are aimed at three- to five-year-olds. Using two coloured pens, maybe red for girls and blue for boys, keep a tally of the number of times each sex shows a behaviour from your list. Write a short report on your findings or produce a short presentation to give to the rest of your group.

Starter activity

1. Most people can think of at least one person they know who holds **prejudiced** views towards another group of people in society. What do you think makes a person prejudiced towards others? Are we born with these views? Do we learn them? If so, from whom and how?

   With a partner, list your ideas and then share them with your group. Are there any common ideas that have emerged? What are they?

Objectives

You will be able to:

define prejudice

define discrimination

describe and evaluate the work of Adorno.

An individual is said to be prejudiced towards another when they have a rigid set of attitudes or beliefs towards that person. This is because of the group they belong to. This attitude or belief is usually negative. If you are prejudiced towards someone, you are prejudging them before you get to know them. Prejudice occurs towards different groups of people for reasons such as age, ethnicity, physical appearance, sexual orientation and where they live. For example, someone living in an expensive part of town may be believed by others to be a snob, despite these people never having met them. Unemployed people often face prejudice. People tend to believe that these people are lazy, when in fact there may be other reasons why the person does not have a job. They are prejudging these people as being lazy despite having never met them.

Discrimination is the way a person behaves towards another because of their prejudiced view. Prejudice is the attitude; discrimination is the resulting behaviour. You discriminate against someone by treating them differently to the way you treat others. Discrimination can involve speaking in a different manner to someone, paying them differently, ignoring them, or using an unfriendly tone of voice with them.

Key terms

Prejudice: a rigid set of attitudes or beliefs towards particular groups of people. These attitudes are usually negative, but not always.

Discrimination: (with reference to prejudice) the way an individual behaves towards another person or group as a result of their prejudiced view. This behaviour is usually negative, but could also be positive.

A TV presenter Selina Scott experienced age discrimination when she was denied the opportunity to cover a maternity leave due to her age

Activity

1. Working with a partner, list at least **four** groups of people in society that may experience prejudice and discrimination. For each of your groups, briefly explain the discrimination they may experience. Feed back and discuss your ideas with other pairs.

Research study

Prejudice

For many years psychologists have been trying to explain why people are prejudiced towards others. It is normally the negative views that they are interested in. There are a range of theories on offer.

Barrett and Short (1992)

Aim: To look at the development of prejudice among young children.

Method: Researchers interviewed 216 English children aged between five and 10 years old, on their views and opinions on people from different European countries.

Results: It was found that, at this age, children already demonstrated more positive views towards some European groups than to others. They found that the Germans were liked the least while the French were liked the most, despite the children having no factual information on these nationalities.

Conclusion: By the age of 10, children already hold prejudiced views towards other nationalities.

Activity

2 List as many reasons as you can why the children in the Barratt and Short study may have held these prejudiced views at such a young age. Compare your list with those of the rest of your group and discuss your reasons.

Discrimination

There are laws in place to prevent employers from discriminating against people applying for jobs. These laws cover racial, sexual, religious, disability and age discrimination. In theory, a person from a minority ethnic group with the same qualifications and experience as a white person applying for the same job should have the same chances. Researchers test this by sending out fake job applications. They will send the same application to the same company. One of the applicants will have a white British-sounding name and the other will have a name from a minority ethnic group. If one is called for interview, so should the other be, if there is no discrimination occurring. The Commission for Racial Equality published a report in 1997, which showed that employers were still discriminating by not inviting people from minority ethnic groups to interviews. This was despite their having the same qualifications on paper as a white applicant.

Activity

3 a Write a short newspaper article about someone who has committed a crime. Look at current newspapers for ideas. Make two copies of your article. Attach a picture of a white British person to one and a picture of someone from a minority ethnic group to the other. Show each article to at least five different people and ask them to choose a prison sentence for the criminal. You may want to give them options ranging from one to 10 years.

   b Find the mean number of years given as a prison sentence for each criminal. Did you find any evidence of discrimination taking place? Write a short report on your study or prepare a presentation to give to the rest of your group.

Going further

1 Search newspapers or the internet for everyday examples where groups are targets of frustration leading to prejudice. Try to explain why this happens for each group.

∞ links

See Topic 5.3 to find out how to calculate the mean.

2 Do this activity on your own. Answer '**agree**' or '**disagree**' for each of the following statements.

a One of the most important things that children should learn is obedience to authority.

b All children need strict discipline.

c All children should learn respect for authority.

d Some professionals in society, such as businessmen, are much more important than others, such as artists.

e If you have a problem, it is best not to think about it. You should keep busy with other more cheerful things.

f If people chatted less and worked more, everyone in society would be better off.

g If people commit serious crimes, such as rape or attacks on children, prison isn't enough. They should be publicly whipped or hung.

h Many of the problems society faces today would be solved if we could somehow get rid of the less intelligent members, homosexuals and the disabled.

i Homosexuals should be considered in the same category as criminals and so should be severely punished.

j If you are not taught manners at an early age, you can hardly expect to mix with decent people later on in life.

Count up the number of questions you answered 'agree' to. The higher the number of 'agrees', the more of an **authoritarian personality** you have. What characteristics do you think make up an authoritarian personality? Discuss this with your group.

Authoritarian personality

Adorno and his colleagues wanted to find out why Nazi soldiers behaved in such atrocious ways towards Jews and other minority groups during the Second World War.

B *German soldiers executing Polish citizens during the Second World War*

Research study

Adorno (1950)

Aim: To find out if there is a relationship between a person's personality type and prejudiced beliefs.

Method: Hundreds of people were interviewed and tested using the **F-scale**.

Results: They found a relationship between personality traits and prejudiced views.

Conclusion: There is an authoritarian personality and people with these characteristics are highly likely to be prejudiced towards others.

According to Adorno's study, personality characteristics that made up the authoritarian personality included:

- disliking Jews
- being resistant to any change, preferring to stick to established routines
- holding traditional values and beliefs
- sticking rigidly to beliefs
- being obedient to those in a higher authority
- looking down on those who are felt to be of a lesser status.

In further research, Adorno found that people with authoritarian personalities were likely to have had parents who were critical and strict.

Activity

5 Discuss Adorno's theory with a partner. Do you agree that a person's personality type is linked to whether they are prejudiced are not? Why or why not? List at least **three** criticisms of Adorno's research. Don't forget to consider the method he used. Don't read on until you have attempted this activity.

Evaluation

There are many criticisms of Adorno's theory:

- The theory doesn't explain why people are prejudiced towards some groups but not others.
- It is difficult to provide evidence to support the idea that parenting style contributes to an authoritarian personality. Evidence for this relies on people's memories, which are not always reliable or accurate.
- There are some prejudiced people in society who didn't grow up with critical and strict parents. Also, there are people in society who grew up with critical and strict parents but are not prejudiced.
- The statements used in the F-scale test have been criticised. It is believed that the statements were easier to agree with than disagree with so they were not a reliable way of measuring people's views.
- The research was done in America, so can it be applied cross-culturally?
- Adorno only found that there was a relationship (correlation) between personality type and prejudice. This cannot show cause and effect.

Despite these criticisms, Adorno's research led the way for other psychologists to develop their theories. Some of these will be examined in the remaining topics of this chapter.

Check your understanding

1 What is meant by the term 'prejudice'? *(2 marks)*

2 What is meant by the term 'discrimination'? *(2 marks)*

3 Explain what is meant by the 'authoritarian personality'. *(3 marks)*

4 Outline **two** criticisms of Adorno's explanation of prejudice. *(4 marks)*

Activity

4 The 10 statements you answered 'agree' or 'disagree' to in the Starter activity were taken from Adorno's F-scale questionnaire. With a partner, list as many criticisms as you can of the statements you responded to. Share your ideas with the rest of your group.

Did you know ??????

Adorno wasn't the only psychologist to conduct research based on the behaviour of Nazi soldiers during the Second World War. Milgram did as well (see Chapter 7).

AQA Examiner's tip

When asked to evaluate a study in an exam, don't forget to consider the positives as well as the negatives. Also, don't forget to consider problems with the methodology, with the sample of participants used, as well as ethical issues.

∞ links

See Topic 10.4 to find out more about correlation.

Going further

2 Go to the website www.anesi.com/fscale.htm and have a go at completing the full version of the authoritarian personality questionnaire.

4.3 Is there prejudice and discrimination between groups?

Starter activity

1 Divide into small teams. You must each have a copy of a puzzle (Sudoku, crossword, word search, spot the difference). You must have a time limit to complete the puzzle in. When the time limit is up, the winning team is the team that has solved the most of the puzzle.

Before you start, your teacher will need to find a desirable prize for the winning team in this activity.

Objectives

You will be able to:

describe and evaluate the work of Sherif

describe and evaluate the work of Tajfel

give explanations of prejudice and discrimination.

Activity

1 Think about the answers to the following questions on your own, then feed back your thoughts and feelings to your group.

a When you were working on the Starter activity, how keen were you to win the prize?

b Did the prize motivate you to try harder?

c Did your team pull together?

d Was there any unpleasantness towards the other teams?

e Were you aware of how well the other teams were doing?

f If you lost, how did you feel? If you won, how did you feel?

g Do you think competition for something that's limited can lead to prejudice developing?

■ Robbers Cave experiment

Sherif was interested in finding out what led people within a society to become prejudiced towards others. He believed that it could be because groups within society were competing for scarce resources. To test his hypothesis he designed an experiment, which he conducted on teenage boys at a summer camp.

Key terms

Robbers Cave: the name given to Sherif's experiment on prejudice.

Research study

Sherif (1961)

Aim: To find out if prejudice develops when groups are in competition for scarce resources.

Method: An American summer camp was organised for 22 boys. The boys were randomly split into two teams and the teams were kept away from each other. They were not aware that the other team existed. The boys were given time to settle into their camps and form a group identity. After a while, the two groups discovered each other and the camp staff introduced a series of competitions with the prize for the winning team being a silver cup.

Results: Very quickly, the teams began unpleasant name-calling towards each other and tried to attack each other.

Conclusion: Competition is a cause of prejudice.

A *Robbers Cave summer camp*

Did you know ??????

Sherif's experiment is called the Robbers Cave experiment because it was conducted in Robbers Cave State Park, Oklahoma, USA.

Additional details

Sherif organised his camp as a typical American summer camp. The boys were aged 12, white and from stable middle-class homes. For the first few days of the camp, normal summer camp activities took place and each group gave themselves a name. One group called themselves 'Rattlers' and the other chose 'Eagles'.

Once the groups became aware of each other, the competitions for the silver cup began. These included the tidiest camp and sporting events. Sherif also arranged situations that left one group gaining at the expense of the other. A picnic was set up and one group was delayed getting there. When they did arrive, there was hardly any food left. Things got so bad between the two groups that camp staff had to break up fights.

AQA *Examiner's tip*

The information on the opposite page and the evaluation of the study are all you would need to learn about Sherif's study for the exam, but the additional details are worth knowing.

Activities

2   Divide a plain piece of A4 or A3 paper into eight equal sections, and number each section from 1 to 8. Re-read Sherif's study and the additional details. Then break down the study into eight sentences. Write one of your sentences in each of the sections on your paper. Now produce a storyboard of Sherif's study, drawing a picture to illustrate each sentence.

3   Divide a piece of paper into two columns; label one column 'Strengths' and the other 'Criticisms'. List as many strengths and criticisms of Sherif's study as you can. Don't read on until you have completed this activity.

Evaluation

- The groups and competitions were artificial and so don't necessarily reflect real life.
- He used 12-year-old, white, middle-class boys. Should the results really be generalised to females, other ages and other social classes?
- The boys were American, therefore we should be careful when generalising to other nationalities.
- It has real-life implications. The study clearly demonstrated how quickly prejudice can arise between groups when they are competing for the same thing.
- It showed how quickly people form alliances with others when they feel they have something in common with them. It also showed how quickly they can turn against others they see as being different to themselves.

AQA *Examiner's tip*

When you are asked to describe a study in your exam, you will normally be expected to give the aim, method, results and conclusion. Only *evaluate* the study if you are specifically asked to do so. Also, read the question carefully because you will not be asked for the aim every time.

Going further

1   Have a look at recent newspapers, listen to the news or search the internet for groups in our society that experience prejudice. Could their situation be explained through Sherif's theory of competition for scarce resources?

2 Do this activity on your own. List at least five groups that you belong to (such as your psychology group, your family, your sports team). List at least five groups you don't belong to (such as a subject group you don't take, a sports team you don't play for). Now go back to your first list and note down at least two things you have in common with the rest of the people in that group. This is your list of **in-groups**. Your second list is your list of **out-groups**.

In-group: a group of people you believe you have something in common with, for example, your psychology group.

Out-group: a group of people whom you believe you have nothing in common with.

Other studies

The groups of people you have things in common with are known as your in-groups. If you study GCSE psychology, are part of a hockey team, support Arsenal football club, enjoy listening to pop music, then your list of in-groups will include these. This means you will feel some sort of allegiance to other members of these groups.

4 Do you think you are more likely to help someone in need if you have something in common with them (they are in one of your in-groups), than if you don't have anything in common with them (they are in an out-group)? Discuss this in pairs and feed back your thoughts to the group.

Research study

Levine (2002)

Aim: To show that, if people believed they had a relationship with a stranger, they would be more likely to help them.

Method: A situation was set up so that a stuntman fell over in front of Manchester United fans. Half the time he was wearing a Manchester United shirt; the rest of the time he was wearing a Liverpool shirt.

Results: When he was wearing the Manchester United shirt, he was helped to his feet every time. However, when he was wearing the Liverpool shirt, he was left to help himself every time.

Conclusion: When we feel we have something in common with others, we are more likely to help them. We are less likely to help out-group members.

B *Out-group individuals may be treated unfavourably by in-group members*

Activity

5 Divide into two teams. Each team needs a team name and access to a copy of the grid below:

18	17	16	15	10	13	12	11	10	9	8	7	6	5
25	6	17	14	12	10	11	12	13	11	15	1	17	18

To play this game, each team takes it in turn to award points to themselves from the top row and points to the other team from the bottom row. The points are in pairs. If the first team choose to give themselves 18 points, the other team would receive 25 points. If the first team gave themselves 7 points, the other team would get 1 point. Teams take their turn alternately. The winning team is the team with the most points after 10 goes.

After the game, discuss how each team decided which point-pairs to award.

Research study

Tajfel (1970)

Aim: To show how easily people discriminate against their out-groups.

Method: 14–15-year-old boys were randomly assigned to two groups. Each boy was given a game to play where he had to award pairs of points, similar to Activity 5. They were told the points could be swapped for prizes at the end.

Results: The boys awarded points by choosing the pairings that created the biggest difference between the groups, not the pairings that gave them the most points.

Conclusion: People will discriminate against others just because they are members of an out-group.

Evaluation

- Tajfel used boys aged 14–15 years old. Should we really generalise the results to females and other ages?
- The groups were artificially created so this doesn't reflect real life. In real life, the groups we belong to mean something to us.
- Other research, using participants of both sexes and all ages, has supported Tajfel's findings. Just assigning people to groups is enough to encourage discriminatory behaviour.

Going further

2 Research the different groups of people that live in your local community. How many different groups are there? Make a presentation or a display about the in-groups and out-groups in your local area.

Check your understanding

1 Outline Sherif's view on the cause of prejudice. *(2 marks)*

2 Evaluate Sherif's study on prejudice. *(3 marks)*

3 Explain Tajfel's theory of in-groups and out-groups. *(3 marks)*

4 Evaluate Tajfel's theory of prejudice. *(3 marks)*

Activity

6 In pairs, list at least **three** evaluative comments on Tajfel's research (these can include strengths and criticisms). Compare and discuss your evaluations with the rest of your group. Don't read the Evaluation until you have attempted this activity.

C *In-groups and out-groups – young football supporters shout abuse at their rivals*

4.4 How can we reduce prejudice and discrimination?

Starter activity

1   State whether each of the following statements is from the theories of Adorno, Tajfel or Sherif:

a   People are prejudiced because of their personality type.

b   People are prejudiced because of competition between groups in society.

c   People are prejudiced because they believe their in-groups are superior to their out-groups.

Objectives

You will be able to:

explain prejudice and discrimination based on the studies covered so far

describe ways of reducing prejudice and discrimination using evidence from the work of Sherif, Aronson, Elliott and Harwood

suggest practical implications of research into prejudice and discrimination.

Explanations of prejudice and discrimination

Activity

1   In pairs or small groups, list situations of prejudice and discrimination that are occurring in the world or have occurred in the past. For each situation on your list, can you explain it in terms of Adorno, Tajfel or Sherif's theories?

So far in this chapter, we have looked at three explanations of prejudice and discrimination:

- Adorno believes you are likely to be prejudiced if you are brought up by strict, critical parents and have an authoritarian personality.
- Sherif believes you are likely to be prejudiced if you are in competition with another group for a scarce resource.
- Tajfel believes you are likely to be prejudiced because you favour your in-groups over your out-groups and believe your in-groups to be superior.

Activity

2   For each of the three explanations of prejudice, think of at least one way in which the explanation could be used to reduce prejudice in society today?

Reducing prejudice and discrimination

Evidence from Sherif (1961)

Once Sherif had created prejudice between the two groups, his next aim was to see if he could get the boys to become friends. He attempted to do this by arranging joint activities for them, such as trips to the cinema and meals out. However, this did not work and the boys continued to attack each other and call each other names. Sherif then set up a situation whereby their truck got stuck in mud and needed pulling out, otherwise they would all miss dinner. This was successful because the task could not be completed without effort from all. Sherif concluded that cooperation on an important task is one way of reducing prejudice between groups.

A   *Sherif's boys cooperating to pull the truck out of the ditch*

Evidence from Aronson (2000)

Aronson was given the task of eliminating prejudice between black and white students in a school in Texas, USA. He developed a technique called the **jigsaw method**, which involved the students being in mixed-race groups, each taking responsibility for a part of the lesson. They had to become experts on their part and then pass on this knowledge to another group of students within the class. The technique proved successful because each student was responsible for their own learning as well as that of others. Aronson interviewed the students afterwards and found that this method had:

- enhanced their self-esteem
- increased their liking of their classmates
- improved their perceptions of the other racial group within the class.

Key terms

Jigsaw method: the name given to the technique used by Aronson to reduce prejudice within a group of mixed-race students.

Expert groups: another name for the jigsaw method. It is called expert groups because each member of the group becomes an expert on a particular topic and they then pass this knowledge on to the rest of their group.

B   *Students from different racial groups working together*

Activity

3 a Divide into small groups, about four students in each and preferably non-friendship groups. Each group has to research a topic, such as abnormal behaviour. Within each group, each member has to learn a subtopic, such as schizophrenia, unipolar disorder, obsessive-compulsive disorder or phobias (for abnormal behaviour).

Each group member must research and learn their part. The set of questions to research could be:

  i   What is it?

  ii What percentage of the population may suffer from it?

  iii How is it diagnosed?

  iv Describe one treatment for it.

  b After a set time, they must communicate what they have learnt to the rest of their group.

  c At the end of the lesson, your teacher will give each student a short test on what they have learnt and will give them their score for the test.

Did you know ??????

Another name for Aronson's jigsaw method is **expert groups**.

2 a Explain how Sherif suggested that prejudice between groups could be reduced.

    b Explain how Aronson suggested that prejudice between groups could be reduced.

Evidence from Elliott (1970)

The morning after Martin Luther King Jr was killed, Jane Elliott was teaching a class of white, nine-year-olds. These children had never met anyone of a different colour to themselves. She wanted to explain to these children about what had happened the night before. She decided that the only way to do this was to let the children experience what it felt like to be judged by a physical characteristic you have no control over. She decided to do this by using the colour of their eyes.

Elliott (1970)

Aim: To teach her class what it felt like to be victims of discrimination.

Method: Elliott told her class the following:

- Blue-eyed children are smarter than those with brown eyes.
- Blue-eyed children are the best people in the room.
- Brown-eyed children cannot play with blue-eyed children in the playground because they are not as good.
- Brown-eyed children cannot use the drinking fountain.

Results: The reaction of the children to these statements was immediate. The blue-eyed children were delighted, arrogant and became vicious. The brown-eyed children were angry, saddened, confused and withdrawn. Fights broke out in the playground between children who had been best friends the day before. The following day, Elliott reversed the experiment. She found the brown-eyed children behaved in the same arrogant way that the blue-eyed children had the previous day. Similarly the blue-eyed children became withdrawn and sad.

Conclusion: Elliott believed that, by getting the children to experience first hand what it felt like to be victims of prejudice and discrimination, these children would grow up being more tolerant towards others.

Research study

Evidence from Harwood (2003)

Harwood (2003)

Aim: To investigate children's views of the elderly.

Method: Harwood asked children and their grandparents about their relationships. The children were also questioned about their views of elderly people in general.

Results: Children who had regular **contact** with grandparents held positive views towards the elderly.

Conclusion: Contact with grandparents is a good predictor of a child's attitude towards the elderly.

Research study

Activity

4 Ask anyone who has blue eyes to put their hand up. Read out the following statements to the group and watch their reactions.

If you have blue eyes, you:

a are cleverer than those with brown eyes

b are the best people in this room

c can leave the lesson a few minutes early

d don't have to do your homework.

Discuss how those with blue eyes felt and how those with brown or green eyes felt as they heard the above statements.

Did you know ??????

You can find out more about Jane Elliott's blue/brown eyes study, and view a video clip of it by visiting her website at: **www.janeelliott.com**

Evaluation

Sherif

Sherif's method may only have been successful because his groups and the prejudice between them were artificially created. However, his method did show that, if two groups work together to achieve a common goal, prejudice can be reduced.

Aronson

Aronson found that his jigsaw method did lead to prejudice between the racial groups being reduced. However, the positive perceptions of the other racial groups were not generalised outside of the classroom.

Elliott

Elliott's research could be considered unethical as the children suffered from psychological stress. However, when she contacted the students nine years later, they were more tolerant and showed more **empathy** towards others, than children who had not experienced her lesson.

Harwood

Information gathered from interviews is not always reliable. There are children who don't have regular contact with grandparents but still have positive attitudes towards the elderly.

Practical implications

- Sherif's theory is difficult to put into practice in real life. There may be tasks in communities that will need groups to work together to complete, but how do you get the groups to join in?
- Aronson's work suggests that within schools and workplaces prejudice could be reduced, but this may not generalise to other settings.
- Elliott's method of creating empathy within her children worked, but you need children to experience this at an early age.
- Harwood's research illustrates the importance of regular contact between children and grandparents.

Check your understanding

1 Sherif, Aronson, Elliott and Harwood all developed methods of reducing prejudice. Draw up a table to match each psychologist to their method:
   a creating empathy
   b the jigsaw method
   c contact with grandparents
   d cooperation between groups. *(2 marks)*

2 Describe **one** study in which the reduction of prejudice was investigated. Include in your answer the reason why the study was conducted, the method used, the results obtained and the conclusion drawn. *(4 marks)*

3 Explain the likely success of prejudice-reduction techniques in everyday life. *(3 marks)*

Activity

5 Copy the following table. Then provide strengths and limitations for each of the theories of how to reduce prejudice and discrimination.

	Strengths of theory	Limitations of theory
Sherif		
Aronson		
Elliott		
Harwood		

Activity

6 In pairs, discuss the practical implications of the research into prejudice and discrimination. Feed back and discuss your suggestions with the rest of your group.

AQA Examiner's tip

Remember that all social psychological studies can be criticised for ethical reasons.

Going further

Now that you have covered everything you need to know for this course about ways of reducing prejudice and discrimination, create a spider diagram that links all this knowledge together.

Do this with a partner and see which pair can produce the most organised and helpful spider diagram.

5 Research methods

5.1 What is the experimental method?

Objectives

You will be able to:

formulate testable hypotheses

understand experimental designs and their advantages and disadvantages

understand the use of standardised procedures

understand the experimental method and its advantages and disadvantages.

Starter activity

1 You need to find out from the members of your group the answer to the following questions:

a How many people in the room listen to music when they are doing their homework?

b How many people think that listening to music makes them work better?

Put the answers up on the board. Discuss what these seem to show for your group.

Procedures in the experimental method

Most psychologists believe that studies of human behaviour should be carried out in scientific settings whenever possible. This means that the researcher will follow the procedures that have been used by all scientists. The most common method used in science is to conduct experiments. The following sections show you how psychologists do this.

Formulating hypotheses

Most research in psychology starts with an idea about something that might be happening and the psychologist wants to test the idea in a scientific way. Sometimes the idea can be quite vague, such as:

Does it affect the way students learn if they are listening to music while doing their work?

The researcher will then try to rewrite the vague idea into a more precise **hypothesis**. This is a testable statement that makes it very clear what the researcher expects to happen. It usually involves a prediction about how one **variable** will affect another variable. For the question about students who listen to music while learning, we need to identify the two variables that we are interested in studying.

The two variables are:

- something to do with whether there is music playing while the studying is happening
- something to do with how well the students learn.

Key terms

Hypothesis: a testable statement about the relationship between two variables. In an experiment these variables are called the independent variable (IV) and the dependent variable (DV).

Variable: a factor or thing that can change – it varies.

A *Studying with music*

Activity

1 Design an experiment to test the idea that there is a difference in how well students learn when they listen to music and when they don't listen to music.

In groups of three or four, discuss what you would do to find out the answer to this problem about music and learning. Use the Key terms box to help you to:

a write the hypothesis

b identify the **independent variable (IV)** and **dependent variable (DV)** for the **experiment**.

You will also need to think about what the people in the experiment will have to do – there must be a task for them. How will you carry out the study? Who should take part and how will they take part?

When you have a plan, present it to the rest of the group and be ready to explain the decisions you have made.

You need to keep your 'music study' information safe as you will return to it throughout this chapter.

Key terms

Independent variable (IV): the variable that the researcher alters or manipulates to look for an effect on another variable. This variable produces the two conditions of the study.

Dependent variable (DV): the variable that the researcher measures to see if the IV has affected it.

Experiment: the method of research in which all variables other than the independent variable (IV) and dependent variable (DV) are controlled. This allows the researcher to identify a cause-and-effect relationship between the IV and DV.

Condition: an experiment is usually organised so there are two trials, after which the performances of the participants are compared. These are the conditions of the experiment.

You have probably realised that the IV, DV, hypothesis and experiment are all related to each other. When you design an experiment you need to identify the IV and DV so that you can then write these in the hypothesis. You can do this by asking yourself to complete the following:

This experiment is looking at the effect of _____ (the IV) on _____ (the DV).

The first gap in the sentence is filled in with the IV or two **conditions** of the experiment that are being altered or manipulated by the experimenter. The second gap will be filled in with the DV or performance of the participants that the experimenter plans to measure.

In the 'music study' experiment, the answer would be:

*This experiment is looking at the effect of **the presence or absence of music** on **the score in a learning test**.*

So the IV is the presence or absence of music and the DV is the score in a learning test.

Once you have identified the IV and DV it is easy to write the hypothesis. A suitable hypothesis for this experiment would be:

The presence or absence of music has an effect on the score in a learning test.

B *Studying without music*

Going further

1 Working in pairs, look back at the experiments described in Chapters 1–4.

See if you can identify the IV and DV in each one.

Discuss your findings with others in your group.

Experimental designs

The term 'experimental design' refers to how the **participants** are used in an experiment. There are usually two conditions in an experiment and the experimenter has to decide who will take part in each condition. There are three experimental designs that can be used:

- **Independent groups** – the available people for the experiment are divided into two groups. One group takes part in one of the conditions of the experiment and the other group takes part in the remaining condition of the experiment. In the 'music study' experiment, one group of people would learn with music present and the other group would learn without music present.

- **Repeated measures** – there is one group of participants. The participants take part in both conditions of the experiment. For the 'music study' experiment, all the participants would learn some material with music and they would also learn some material without music.

- **Matched pairs** – the available people for the experiment are tested before taking part and are matched for qualities into pairs. They could be identified as Pair **Aa**, Pair **Bb** and so on. One member of the pair takes part in one condition of the study (that group comprises **A**, **B**, **C**, and so on). The other member takes part in the other condition (that group comprises **a**, **b**, **c**, and so on). Identical twins are often considered to be perfect matched pairs in psychology research.

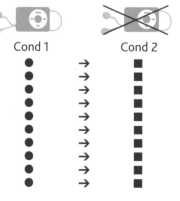

C *A matched pair?*

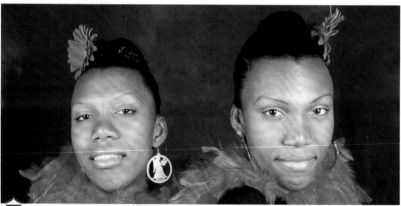

Independent groups		Repeated measures		Matched pairs	
Cond 1	Cond 2	Cond 1	Cond 2	Cond 1	Cond 2
●	■	● →	■	A	a
●	■	● →	■	B	b
●	■	● →	■	C	c
●	■	● →	■	D	d
●	■	● →	■	E	e
●	■	● →	■	F	f
●	■	● →	■	G	g
●	■	● →	■	H	h
		● →	■		

D *Three possible experimental designs*

Activity

2 Using the information about experimental designs, think about which experimental designs could be used for your 'music study' experiment.

What would be the advantages and disadvantages of each design for the experiment? Which would you use and why?

Share your answers with the rest of your group.

Add this information to your 'music study' notes.

Key terms

Order effect: this occurs when a participant's performance in the second condition of an experiment is affected because they have already done the first condition. They may do better because of practice or worse because of tiredness. This may happen in a repeated measures design.

Participant variables: the differences between the people who take part in the study. These may affect the results of an experiment that uses an independent groups design.

Advantages and disadvantages of different experimental designs

These can be summarised in the table below.

E   *Experimental designs: advantages and disadvantages*

	Advantages	Disadvantages
Independent groups	• There are no **order effects** because people only take part in one condition. • Often the same material can be used for the task in both conditions. • Participants cannot work out the aim of the study because they only take part in one condition.	• There are different people (participant variables) in the two conditions so that may be why the results are different. • You need more people for the study. To get 10 in each group you need 20 people.
Repeated measures	• The people in both conditions are the same so there are no participant variables. • You only need 10 people to get 20 results because each person produces two 'scores'.	• There are order effects as people have to do two tasks. • You may need two tasks (they cannot learn the same list twice). • Participants may work out the aim of the study because they take part in both conditions.
Matched pairs	• Participant variables are reduced. • There are no order effects. • Often the same material can be used for the task in both conditions.	• Matching is difficult, time-consuming and not always successful. • Some participant variables are still present.

Standardised procedures in experiments

As you have seen, an experiment is a carefully organised procedure. With **standardised procedure**, a set sequence applies to all the participants when necessary. This makes the experiment unbiased. An important issue is how participants in a study are put into the conditions of the experiment. When the design is independent groups, the experimenter can use **random allocation** to achieve this. If 20 people are available for the study, the experimenter can put 10 pieces of paper with 'A' on them and 10 with 'B' into a bag. Each participant takes a piece of paper from the bag and that determines the condition they take part in.

When the experimental design is repeated measures, all the participants have to take part in both conditions. We have seen that this might cause order effects. In order to even these out, a procedure called **counterbalancing** is used. This means half of the participants complete Condition One then Condition Two; the other half complete Condition Two then Condition One. This will not get rid of order effects completely but it may share the effects between the two conditions.

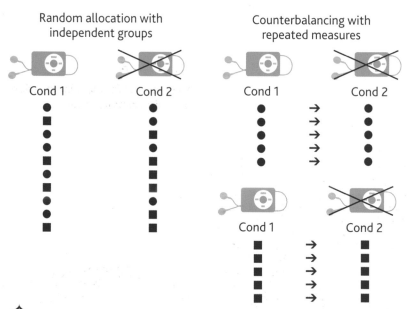

F Two possible ways of putting the participants of a study into the conditions of the experiment

Extraneous variables (EVs) are variables other than the IV that might affect the DV if they are not **controlled**. If we go back to the 'music study' experiment then EVs are things other than the presence or absence of music (IV) that might affect the learning score (DV). Possible problems could be:

- **time allowed to do the test** – if participants in the 'music present condition' have more time than those in the 'music absent condition', then that could affect the scores in the test. The solution would be to allocate the same amount of time for doing the test to both conditions.

- **questions in the test** – if participants in the 'music present condition' have easier questions than those in the 'music absent condition', then that could affect the scores in the test. One solution would be to use the same questions in both conditions.

There are two more issues that an experimenter must consider when standardising procedures. The first concerns the **instructions**, the spoken and written information given to participants to make sure they know what to do. The second concerns how to avoid biases by using a method called 'randomisation' (this is covered on the next page).

Instructions

The information that is said or written for participants might affect the way they do the study and therefore their scores or performances. That could be an EV. The usual practice is to write as much of this information as possible and ensure each participant receives the same information. This is usually done in sections:

- **Briefing** – this is what is said to encourage a person to agree to participate. It contains ethical information about consent, anonymity, the right to withdraw and so on.
- **Standardised instructions** – these are clear instructions about exactly what the participant will have to do in the experiment.
- **Debriefing** – this explains the study in detail so that each participant is absolutely sure of the aim of the study, why they were doing what they were doing in the condition(s). Ethical issues are addressed again, especially the opportunity for the participant to withdraw their data if they feel unhappy about their performance.

G *Briefing and debriefing – essential parts of standardised procedures*

Activity

3 In pairs, work out why having the same questions in both conditions would not be an appropriate solution in a repeated measures design. What would you do in this case?

Key terms

Instructions: the written (or verbal) information given to participants during the experiment.

∞ links

See Topic 5.4 for more information on ethical considerations.

Did you know ?????

In any experiment it is likely that some participants will be more excited about taking part than others and there will be differences in intelligence and experience. These minor differences can cause a *random error* in the results – an error that occurs by chance. Using large numbers of participants means that these errors cancel each other out, making the results more reliable.

Activity

4 For your 'music study' experiment, you should now consider the issues of EVs and instructions:

a   Identify at least **two** EVs that might affect your experiment. Explain what effect these could have and how you would control each EV.

b   Write the instructions for participants in your experiment. Remember, you have three sections to complete. You must refer to the ethical considerations in Topic 5.4 on pages 82–3 before the instructions can be completed.

c   Add this information to your 'music study' work.

Standardised procedures in experiments (continued)

Randomisation

Another technique used in practical work is called **randomisation**. This means making sure that, where necessary, there are no biases in procedures.

This might, for example, be used when the experimenter has constructed a list of 20 words for participants to learn. These words are of equal difficulty because they are all everyday nouns with six letters. The experimenter has to decide the order in which they should be presented to the participants. Instead of the experimenter choosing the order, randomisation is used. All 20 words are written on separate pieces of paper and put in a bag. The first word is pulled out of the bag and written down at the top of the list. This is repeated until all 20 words have been put on the list. The order of words has now been *randomised*. Each word had an equal chance of being selected first for the list and the experimenter left the final order of the words to chance.

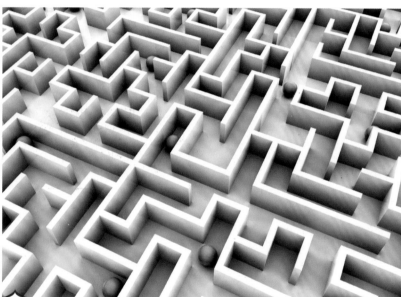

H *Don't get lost in a maze – keep all your procedures organised*

Research in natural and experimental settings

As you have seen, psychological research in experimental settings is a scientific, controlled approach to finding out about human behaviour. There are many benefits to conducting research in this way. However, when the setting is natural, there is more evidence that the behaviour produced is real human behaviour and a true reflection of what people really do. This relates to the issue of **ecological validity**. An experimenter may set up an investigation that requires people to become participants and perform a specially designed task in timed conditions. The problem is that the behaviour and results may not be applicable to real human behaviour. On the other hand, watching people as they go about their daily life would give an ecologically valid account of behaviour.

Key terms

Randomisation: using chance to produce an order for a procedure.

Ecological validity: the results of the investigation can be said to apply to real-life behaviour. They are an accurate account of behaviour in the real world.

Objectivity: not affected by personal biases.

Going further

2 Working in pairs, look back at the experiments in Chapters 1–4.

See if you can identify any that lack ecological validity and say why.

Discuss your findings with others in your group.

∞ links

See Topic 10.2 for information on observation studies.

■ Advantages and disadvantages of experiments

It is important to remember that there are many advantages, as well as disadvantages, to the experimental method. There is no best way of finding out about human behaviour, so researchers choose the most appropriate method for their investigations.

Advantages

- The control of EVs in an experiment means it is easier to identify *the cause and the effect*. This means the experimenter can be more certain that it was the IV that affected the DV.
- Experiments are controlled and standardised so they can be replicated by other researchers (i.e. redone to check that the results are a real effect and not a fluke).
- Experiments are **objective** because the procedures are set up in such a way that biases from the researcher are not present.

Disadvantages

- The settings for experiments can be very artificial. The tasks can be unrealistic (e.g. we rarely memorise word lists). There can be a lack of ecological validity. It is possible to overcome this by using more natural settings for experiments.
- Participants usually know they are in an experiment and this could affect the behaviour they produce. The results could be untrue and misleading because the behaviour was not normal.

Activity

5 Revise the experimental method by copying and completing the following passage and filling in the gaps using some of these terms:

ethical, issues, control, dependent variable, ecological validity, random allocation, hypothesis, independent variable, scientific

Psychologists often choose the experimental method because it is a _____ approach to finding out about human behaviour. It enables the researcher to establish cause and effect because an _____ is manipulated to cause a change in the _____ .The experimenter will _____ extraneous variables. Experiments do have some disadvantages. They are often criticised because the tasks can lack _____ .

AQA *Examiner's tip*

Make sure you don't confuse 'random allocation' and 'randomisation'.

Check your understanding

1 Describe how an experimenter could use counterbalancing in a study where participants are all timed sorting cards:

a in the presence of an audience – Condition A

b in the absence of an audience – Condition B. *(3 marks)*

2 Identify the IV and DV in the experiment outlined in Question 1. *(2 marks)*

3 Identify a possible EV in the experiment outlined in Question 1. Explain how the EV could be controlled. *(3 marks)*

Going further

3 You might find it useful to draw up a chart on which you organise your understanding of the advantages and disadvantages (or limitations) of experiments and research in natural settings. This will help you to revise for the Unit 1 examination.

5.2 — What are sampling methods?

Starter activity

Go back to your notes on the 'music study' experiment in Topic 5.1 (on the effect of the presence or absence of music on learning test scores).

You have already started to think about the experimental design you could use: either independent groups or repeated measures. You now need to consider where you will get the people from to take part in the experiment. Discuss this in a group and then share your ideas with the other groups. Record the ideas in your notes and keep them for later.

Objectives

You will be able to:

understand sampling methods

understand the advantages and limitations of sampling methods.

Key terms

Participant: a person who is selected to take part in a study.

Sample: the small group of people who represent the target population and who are studied.

Target population: the large group of people the researcher wishes to study.

Representative: the sample of participants is made up of people who have the same characteristics and abilities as the target population.

Generalised: the results from the sample can be said to apply to the target population.

Random sample: every member of the target population has an equal chance of being selected for the sample.

Opportunity sample: people who are members of the target population and are available and willing to take part.

■ Target populations and samples

When psychologists conduct research, they are interested in finding out how people behave in certain situations. What they cannot do is test every person to find this out. Instead, the research is carried out using small groups of people. The people who take part in an investigation are the **participants** and as a group they are the **sample** for the study. The small sample of participants will be selected from a much larger group called the **target population**.

The important issue for the researcher is that the sample of people in a study is **representative** of the target population. If they are, then the researcher can assume that the behaviour of the sample matches the behaviour of the target population. This means that the results of the study can be **generalised** in that the results can be said to apply to not just the sample but to the target population as a whole.

■ Sampling methods

Random

In a **random sample** every member of the target population has an equal chance of being selected for the sample. This means the researcher must identify all the members of the target population, number each person and then draw out the required number of people. If the target population is small, then all the numbers can go into a hat to be drawn out. If it is large, then a computer programme can be used to do this. This sampling method is fair and not biased because the researcher cannot choose the individual participants. However, the sample might not be representative because, for example, the researcher could draw out too many females just by chance.

Opportunity

Opportunity sampling means choosing people who are members of the target population and are available and willing to take part. Often these people are friends of the researcher so they may not represent the target population very well. This could produce a biased sample. The chosen participants may also try to 'help' the researcher by behaving in ways that support the hypothesis being tested, so their results could be unreliable. However, it is a quick and easy way to collect people for a study.

Systematic

Systematic sampling involves selecting every nth member of the target population. For example, if the researcher decides that 'n' will be '7', every 7th person in the target population is selected. This is unbiased because the researcher cannot choose the individuals.

Stratified

Stratified sampling is the most complex of the sampling methods. The researcher must identify the subgroups in the target population and work out what proportion of that target population each group represents. For example, in a school there are several subgroups: teachers, other staff, students in each year, and so on. If the teachers make up 10 per cent of the whole school target population then 10 per cent of the sample must be teachers. This is repeated for each subgroup. Once the researcher knows what proportion needs to be selected for the sample, a random sample of each subgroup is taken. This is very time-consuming. However, it will provide an unbiased and very representative sample of people for the study.

A *Summary of the advantages and limitations of sampling methods*

Sampling method	Advantages	Limitations
Random	No researcher bias Likely to be representative	Time-consuming
Opportunity	Quick and easy	Not likely to be representative and may have researcher bias
Systematic	Simple procedure with no researcher bias	Sample may not be representative
Stratified	Very representative	Very time-consuming

Going further

You should always consider the sampling method used in research that you read about in psychology. This can have implications for the results of the study.

If you have studied some topics already you might like to refer back to the research you learned about and further investigate the sampling method used and its possible effect on the results.

If you have not studied any topics yet, remember this issue when you do start.

Check your understanding

1 A researcher used an opportunity sample to collect participants for his investigation. Identify **one** problem with this method and explain how it could be overcome. *(3 marks)*

2 Outline what is meant by random sampling and give a practical example of how a random sample could be achieved. *(4 marks)*

Key terms

Systematic sample: every 'nth' member of the target population is selected for the sample.

Stratified sample: to obtain this type of sample, the different subgroups in the target population are identified; then people are randomly selected from these subgroups in proportion to their numbers in the target population.

Activity

Once again you will need your notes from the 'music study' experiment in Topic 5.1. Who will be your target population in the music/no music and learning experiment? Which sampling method will you choose and why would it be appropriate?

Make a note of your decisions and discuss the choices you have made with others.

At this point you will need to refer to the ethical considerations in Topic 5.4 on pages 82–3, if you have not already thought about ethics and the age of your participants.

AQA Examiner's tip

You will only gain credit for answers about advantages and limitations of sampling methods if the points you make apply to the method you are discussing.

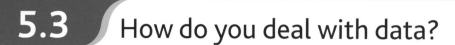

5.3   How do you deal with data?

Starter activity

A researcher set up a study in which six people each solved a puzzle in a room alone and a different group of six people each solved the same puzzle in front of an audience. He compared the average times taken to solve the puzzle when people were alone and in the presence of an audience.

The following data were collected in this experiment.

- Condition A: Time taken to solve the puzzle without an audience (in seconds) 23, 19, 24, 47, 23, 20

- Condition B: Time taken to solve the puzzle with an audience (in seconds) 45, 44, 43, 44, 46, 48

What have you noticed about the times in the two conditions? Discuss ways of analysing the data from the experiment so that any patterns in the data can be seen.

Objectives

You will be able to:

use descriptive statistics to analyse data collected in an investigation

recognise anomalous results

present data graphically.

A   *The audience watches*

■ Data analysis

The data above are in the form of *times taken to solve a puzzle (in seconds)*. This is called the **raw data**. However, researchers usually want to identify patterns in behaviour rather than concentrate on the individual performances. The various means of summarising data are outlined below.

Calculating averages

There are three types of average that can be calculated: mean, mode and median. Each of these averages will be calculated using the data from the Starter activity.

Mean

The **mean** is calculated by adding together all the values in a set of scores and then dividing the total by the number of values in the set.

Key terms

Raw data: the scores collected in a study that have not been analysed or summarised.

Mean: a statistic calculated by adding all the scores in a set of values and dividing the total by the number of values in the set.

Condition A:

mean = 23 + 19 + 24 + 47 + 23 + 20 = 156 (total number of seconds) ÷ 6 (number of values) = **26**

Condition B:

mean = 45 + 44 + 43 + 44 + 46 + 48 = 270 (total number of seconds) ÷ 6 (number of values) = **45**

Mode

The **mode** is the most frequently occurring value in a set of scores. Sometimes there is no mode and sometimes there is more than one mode.

Key terms

Mode: the most frequently occurring value in a set of values.

Condition A:

23, 19, 24, 47, **23**, 20   The mode is **23**.

Condition B:

45, **44**, 43, **44**, 46, 48   The mode is **44**.

Median

The **median** is the middle value in a set of scores. To find the median you must arrange all the values in order from lowest to highest. Then you must find the middle value. If there is no middle value because you have an even number of values, then find the *midpoint* of the *two middle values*.

Condition A:

23, 19, 24, 47, 23, 20 arranged in order, becomes:

19, 20, **23**, **23**, 24, 47. The midpoint of 23 and 23 is **23** so the median is **23**.

Condition B:

45, 44, 43, 44, 46, 48 arranged in order, becomes:

43, 44, **44**, **45**, 46, 48. The midpoint of 44 and 45 is **44.5** so the median is **44.5**.

Calculating the range

Another statistic that can be calculated and used to describe the data is the **range**. This is the numerical difference between the lowest and highest value in a set of scores.

Condition A: the range is 47 − 19 = **28**

Condition B: the range is 48 − 43 = **5**

Key terms

Median: the middle value in a set of values when the values have been arranged in ascending order.

Range: the difference between the lowest and highest value in a set of values.

Activity

1   You now need to conduct your 'music study' experiment to investigate the effect of the presence or absence of music on the score in a learning test and collect data that can be analysed.

Your teacher will discuss with you whether you should all follow the same design using the same task – in this case you could collect data from just one or two participants each. Alternatively, you could work in small groups on a design you have agreed together, or each of you could work as an individual.

You will have to design a learning task that the participants have to complete with or without music, and a recall task so that you have a score for each participant.

You should read Topic 5.4 before completing your preparation for the experiment (see Activity 2 on page 83).

Your teacher will check your design(s) before you carry out the investigation.

When you have the data, calculate the mean, mode, median and range for both conditions.

This is your opportunity to put your understanding into operation.

AQA **Examiner's tip**

When you are asked to describe the results of a study, you should look for patterns in the data. For example, the participants in Condition A (without an audience) solved the puzzle faster than those in Condition B (with an audience). We can see this because the mean time for Condition A was much lower than that for Condition B.

Data and how to deal with it

Anomalous results and their possible effects

If one of the values in a set of scores is extremely high or low then it is called an **anomalous result**. It is a result that does not match the rest of the values in a set of scores. Anomalous results can have a large effect on the mean value and the range for a set of scores. This can be shown using the data for Condition A in the Starter activity. One participant took 47 seconds to solve the puzzle without an audience. This was much longer than the time taken by the other participants in the same condition. The effect on the mean and the range is to increase the values of these statistics.

When a researcher notices an anomalous result, they usually try to offer a sensible explanation for that result. In the Starter activity, it could be that, even without the presence of an audience, the participant was extremely anxious about the task. It is possible they found it difficult to complete because of increased stress levels.

Percentages

A **percentage** is a way of expressing a fraction of a hundred, so 45/100 is 45 per cent. In psychology the frequency of events (the number of times something happens) is sometimes shown as a percentage. For example, researchers collected the data shown in Table **B** from watching 20 boys and 20 girls playing in a school playground.

 B *Play behaviours in young children*

	Categories of behaviours			
	Running	**Hopping**	**Skipping**	**Standing**
Boys	15	2	1	2
Girls	3	8	8	1

This could be presented as a table of percentages.

Calculate percentages in the following way:

Boys running: $\dfrac{\text{Number of observations in category} \times 100}{\text{Total number of observations}}$

Boys running: $\dfrac{15 \times 100}{20} = 75\%$

When all the other percentages are calculated the table would be as in Table **C**.

C *Play behaviours in young children (expressed as percentages)*

	Percentages for each category of behaviour			
	Running (%)	**Hopping (%)**	**Skipping (%)**	**Standing (%)**
Boys	75	10	5	10
Girls	15	40	40	5

⊂⊃ **links**

See Topic 10.3 for information on case studies.

Graphs

The data collected in investigations can often be presented as a graph. Remember, graphs should summarise data so you should not draw graphs that contain the raw data from a study.

Bar chart

A bar chart can be used to display data that are in categories. Each bar represents a separate category and the categories are labelled on the *x*-axis (horizontal). The frequency or amount for each category is on the *y*-axis (vertical.) Each bar should be drawn separated from the next bar – they should not touch.

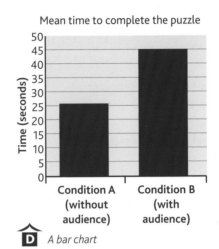

Mean time to complete the puzzle

D   *A bar chart*

Line graph

A line graph is often used to display data that are connected to each other. Joining the points shows that there is a relationship between each point.

It has been shown that a hungry cat placed in a puzzle box will explore and try to escape. Once it has escaped for the first time, the time taken to escape steadily decreases on the following days. The animal learns how to escape. Graph **E** shows the time (in seconds) taken by a cat to escape from a puzzle box on each of five consecutive days.

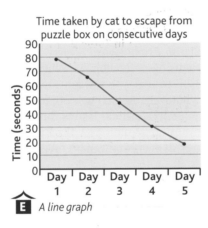

Time taken by cat to escape from puzzle box on consecutive days

E   *A line graph*

Activity

2   Draw a bar chart to represent the percentage data collected in the observation of children playing. Remember to label the axes correctly and provide a suitable heading for your graph.

Activity

3   a   You should now be able to produce a suitable graph to display the results for your music and learning experiment.

b   Write a conclusion to your study that describes the results. What have you discovered about the effect of music on learning? Are there any changes you could make to the experiment to improve it?

c   Discuss these points with the rest of your group.

Check your understanding

1   Calculate the mean, mode and median for the following set of values:
21, 17, 6, 16, 14, 17, 15, 20. *(3 marks)*

2   What is meant by the term 'anomalous data'? *(2 marks)*

3   Draw a bar chart to represent the data shown in the table below. *(4 marks)*

	Activities observed in a gym (%)			
	Treadmill	Rowing machine	Cross trainer	Weights
Men	75	10	5	10
Women	15	40	40	5

links

See Topic 6.2 for more about the cat experiment.

Going further

The mean, median and mode are all types of average. Find out what the differences are between them and see if you can work out when each might be more useful than the others.

Starter activity

Imagine you are being asked to take part in a psychology experiment.

a What would you want to know about the study before you participate?

b How would you like to be treated during the experiment?

c Would you be willing to experience something unpleasant for the 'greater good'?

d What would you want to know about the data collected in the experiment?

In groups of three or four, discuss these issues. Make notes of your discussion so that you can contribute to a whole-group discussion.

If you have studied any particular research that you would not like to have been in, explain why you feel this way.

■ Code of Ethics

The *Code of Ethics and Conduct of the British Psychological Society* (2006) underpin the activities of all practising psychologists. When you conduct any practical work for your GCSE course, you too are covered by this code so you must ensure that, whatever research you do, it is ethical. This means you need to understand the **ethical issues** that relate to your practical work and make sure that you follow the **British Psychological Society (BPS) Guidelines** in everything that you do.

Going further

1 The full code can be found on the BPS website www.bps.org.uk (search for 'code of ethics').

Activity

1 a How should a psychologist deal with the ethical issues described here when conducting research?

b Discuss with your group practical ways of dealing with ethical issues.

Respect

Psychologists should ***respect*** people as individuals and avoid unfair or prejudiced practices. The data collected should be *confidential* so people cannot be identified in the research. This can be especially important in cases studies.

Participants should give *informed consent*. This means they should know what they are consenting to and they must be told what the study is about before they agree to take part. There are special issues when participants are under 16. They should be asked to give their own consent, if that is appropriate. It is important to note that consent

Objectives

You will be able to:

understand ethical issues as outlined by the British Psychological Society Guidelines

understand ways of dealing with these issues.

Key terms

Ethical issues: points of concern about what is morally right.

British Psychological Society (BPS) Guidelines: the ethical guidelines produced by the British Psychological Society in its *Code of Ethics and Conduct* (2006) that govern the work of all practising and research psychologists and also of psychology students in the UK.

A　*Guards are in a position of power*

Did you know ??????

The Stanford Prison experiment was conducted in 1971 (reported in Haney, Banks and Zimbardo, 1973). One group of students were guards and the other group were prisoners. The experiment had to be stopped after six days because the 'guards' became sadistic and the 'prisoners' became withdrawn and depressed.

∞ links

See Topic 10.3 for more about case studies.

from parents, or guardians or someone acting in the place of a parent, like a teacher at school, is also required. If people are being observed in public places their *privacy* should be respected.

Psychologists should avoid *deception*, which means people should not be misled about the research. However, the BPS does recognise that some research would be impossible if everything was revealed at the start. This means researchers must inform participants as soon as possible about any minor deception that has taken place. It would be acceptable to ask people to take part in a 'memory study' and tell them later that it was to investigate the effect of organised and randomised word lists on the number of words recalled.

Finally, participants have the *right to withdraw* from the research at any time and can withdraw their data too.

Competence

Psychologists should only give advice if they are qualified to do so. Certainly, GCSE students must recognise that they have no qualification for giving advice.

Responsibility

Researchers must *protect the participants from harm*. The risk of harm from participation in psychology research should be no greater than the risk from everyday life. The psychological and physical health of participants should not be at risk.

Participants should be *debriefed* at the end of the investigation to ensure they understand fully the true aim of the research.

Integrity

Psychologists should behave with honesty and fairness in all their interactions with all people.

It is essential that psychologists consider whether the benefits of the research can be said to outweigh the possible costs to participants in that research.

links

See Topic 10.2 for more about observation studies.

AQA *Examiner's tip*

In an examination question, make sure that an ethical issue you identify is appropriate for the study described. You should name the issue, such as 'right to withdraw', then explain why it is an issue and how it could be dealt with.

Going further

2 a Working in twos or threes, choose a study from Chapters 1–4.

   b Try to identify possible ethical issues with the study you have chosen. Think about the four aspects described here: respect, competence, responsibility and integrity.

   c When you have finished, share your ideas with the rest of your group.

3 There are some studies in psychology that have caused a great deal of concern because of the way participants were treated. You should research these. Some names to get you started are Stanley Milgram and Philip Zimbardo. Find out what they did and then discuss whether you think the research was justified or not.

Activity

2 You need to apply this information on ethical issues to the experiment you are to carry out into the effect of music on learning.

   Look at the instructions you produced (all the written information you want to present to your participants). Identify the ethical issues you need to consider and add these to your briefing, standardised instructions and debriefing.

Check your understanding

1 Identify **one** ethical issue. Explain why it is an issue and how it could be dealt with. *(3 marks)*

2 Explain why researchers have to take special care when they wish to investigate the behaviour of young children. *(4 marks)*

6 Learning

6.1 What is classical conditioning?

Starter activity

1 What do we mean when we say we have learnt something? Read the statements below and identify which of the following behaviours you think are examples of learning.

a A dog barking when his owner starts to open a can of dog food

b A cat climbing a tree

c A dog chasing a rabbit across a field

d A child sneezing in the sunlight

e A cat using a litter tray

f A child eating with a knife and fork

Objectives

You will be able to:

define learning

define classical conditioning

understand the principles of classical conditioning and the contributions of Pavlov.

Hopefully, you decided that only statements a, e and f are examples of behaviours that are learnt. The others are behaviours that occur naturally; they do not have to be learnt.

For **learning** to occur, there has to be a change in behaviour. An activity that could not be performed previously can now be done because of a particular experience. Try Activity 1 to discover one way that learning might occur.

Key terms

Learning: a relatively permanent change in behaviour due to experience.

Going further

1 There are a number of reflex responses humans produce. These include the *eye blink* and the *knee jerk*. Can you think of any others? Look them up using the internet.

Classical conditioning

One of the earliest explanations of how animals and humans can learn was proposed by Pavlov (1927). He noticed that when the dog he was studying heard the food buckets being brought, it started to salivate (its mouth watered). He knew that salivation is a reflex response; it is an automatic response that should usually occur when food is in the mouth. So, Pavlov realised that the dogs had learnt to salivate to a new event – the sound of the food buckets. This encouraged him to investigate whether dogs could learn to salivate to other events.

Pavlov set up a series of trials over the next few days. Each time the dog was fed, a bell was rung for a few seconds and the amount of saliva produced was measured. Then the bell was rung and no food was given. He discovered that the amount of saliva produced on this trial was the same as when food was given.

Activity

1 For this activity you will need a straw, a bell and someone to be your partner. Sit next to your partner. Your partner should face the front and you need to turn so that you are sitting sideways on. First you will ring a bell and then, using the straw, blow air on to the side of your partner's face, near to the eye. Do this several times (ring bell, blow air; ring bell, blow air...). Then, ring the bell but do not blow any air. Did you notice anything?

Each time air is blown near to your partner's eye, they should blink. When you ring the bell but don't blow air, they should still blink. Why do you think this happens?

A *Pavlov and his dog*

Pavlov gave parts of his procedure special names:

- **Unconditioned** is the term used to show that something is unlearned.
- **Conditioned** means that something has been learned.

The procedure of **classical conditioning** demonstrates a special kind of learning. This is *learning by association*. During the conditioning trials, two stimuli are associated together. The procedure (the **classical conditioning schedule**) is shown in Diagram **B**.

B *Classical conditioning schedule*

Before conditioning trials begin – a reflex	Food UCS	Salivation UCR
During conditioning trials	Bell + Food CS UCS	Salivation UCR
After conditioning	Bell CS	Salivation CR

Pavlov then tried other procedures to investigate, for example, how long the learning would last. He discovered that if he continued to ring the bell without giving the dog any food, after a short time the dog would no longer salivate. He called this **extinction**. Then, after a short period during which no bell had been rung, Pavlov would suddenly ring the bell and the dog would immediately salivate again. He called this response **spontaneous recovery**.

In another series of trials, Pavlov found that, if he changed the tone of the bell, the dog would still salivate. He said that this was **generalisation** because the animal was widening its learned response, the conditioned response (CR) to a similar conditioned stimulus (CS), a new bell sound. Finally, Pavlov discovered that he could stop generalisation in the following way. He rang a number of bells of different tones, but he presented food only when a particular bell was rung. The dog stopped salivating at all the other bells and only salivated when the bell that had been reinforced by food was rung. Pavlov said this was **discrimination** because the dog had learnt to narrow its response to a particular stimulus.

Starter activity

2 Here are five of the terms associated with classical conditioning. Can you match them up with the correct definition (see 1–5, below)?

a Spontaneous recovery

b Extinction

c Conditioned stimulus

d Discrimination

e Unconditioned response.

Copy out these statements and write the correct letter next to each one.

1 A response that has been conditioned no longer appears.

2 A reflex response that occurs naturally without learning.

3 A CR suddenly reappears.

4 A novel or new stimulus that is associated with the UCS.

5 The CR is only produced when a particular stimulus is presented.

Research study

Watson and Rayner (1920)

Aim: To see if the emotional response of fear could be conditioned in a human being.

Method: Albert was 11 months old. He seemed to like a white laboratory rat and had no fear of any white furry objects. In the conditioning trials the rat was shown to Albert and, as he reached for it, a metal bar was hit very hard with a hammer, behind Albert's back. This was done several times.

Results: After seven times, when the rat was presented again, Albert screamed and tried to get away. He did this even though the bar was not hit by the hammer and there was no loud noise. Albert also screamed when he was shown a Santa Claus mask and a fur coat.

Conclusion: Watson and Rayner showed that fear responses could be learnt and even very young children could learn in the way suggested by classical conditioning.

Going further

2 There is a special form of learning that is related to classical conditioning called the Garcia effect. It happens when learning occurs after one pairing of the stimulus and response. An everyday example could be 'you eat a prawn, you are sick, you never eat a prawn again'. The learning is very quick (one trial) and very resistant to extinction (you never forget the connection). Look up the Garcia effect and one-trial learning for other examples of this type of classical conditioning.

Activity

3 What do you think of the Watson and Rayner study? Work with a partner to try to think of at least three criticisms (evaluations). These don't all have to be negative; you might have positive things to say about the study. Don't read on until you have completed this activity.

Activity

2 It is easy to see how it might be possible to condition a dog to salivate in the way that Pavlov did in his research, but can you think of any behaviours that you or your friends do that could be conditioned? Remember, a conditioned response started out as a reflex – something that you automatically do, but now you do it in a more novel situation. Compare your ideas with others'.

C Fear can be conditioned

Did you know ??????

There are lots of ways that people have used classical conditioning to change behaviour. Have you heard of the new device called a 'mosquito'? This is a machine that sends out a high-pitched signal that most young people can hear and find very uncomfortable. These devices have been put up in places where young people meet, near shops or on street corners. It works in the following way: young people hear the sound, find it very annoying and therefore move away from the area where the device has been placed. In classical conditioning terms, the young people have learnt to associate the place with the horrible sound and learn not to go there again.

Evaluation of Watson and Rayner's study

- You might have said that this was not a very ethical thing for the researchers to do to a small child.
- This study only involved one child and maybe the researchers needed more evidence that fear can be learnt in this way. However, the study certainly seems to fit with what you might already know about any phobia that you might have.

Practical applications of classical conditioning

In everyday life, advertising agencies recognise that if they can get us to build up a favourable association between the advert and the product, then we might buy that product more often. Look at Photo **D**.

You probably don't know him by name, but you might remember him singing about the products of the company he worked for. He became very popular and it is possible that people came to associate the fact that they like him, with the idea that they liked the company he represented. Certainly, that is what advertising companies hope to achieve when they use famous people to promote products. They want the audience to associate the 'attractive/nice' person with the brand they are selling.

D *Do you recognise this person?*

∞ links

See Topic 5.4 for more on ethics in psychological research.

AQA Examiner's tip

If you are asked to explain how a particular type of learning (such as a fear response) might happen through classical conditioning, you should draw a classical conditioning schedule to help you. The new learning is the bottom line of the schedule: the CS–CR association. You then need to work out when the response usually occurs. That means asking yourself, 'When does this response usually happen?' That will help you to complete the schedule.

Group activity 🔲🔲🔲🔲

In a small group, try to think of ways that classical conditioning procedures might be used in the real world, for example, in advertising or health promotions. You might like to do some research into a specific campaign and its success and then present your ideas to the rest of your group.

Check your understanding

1   Outline what is meant by the term 'learning'. *(2 marks)*

2   Explain what is meant by 'generalisation' and 'discrimination'. *(4 marks)*

3   Sally, who is 10, is afraid of balloons. Every time she sees a balloon she screams and runs away. When she was younger, a balloon popped in her face. Use the classical conditioning schedule to work out why Sally now reacts the way she does whenever she sees a balloon. *(4 marks)*

6.2   What is operant conditioning?

Starter activity

1. Can you think of any other ways that humans might learn? Remember, classical conditioning suggests that learning occurs when a reflex response is associated with a new stimulus. Do you think that people learn to speak French or drive a car in the same way that Pavlov's dogs learned to salivate at the sound of a bell? How did you learn to do your homework on time?

Objectives

You will be able to:

define operant conditioning

explain Thorndike's Law of Effect and the contributions of Skinner

understand the principles of operant conditioning and the contributions of Skinner.

A

Activity

1. List some of the things that people could do to encourage you to:

   a   tidy your bedroom

   b   help with the washing up

   c   complete your homework on time.

Law of Effect

Operant conditioning is learning that takes place because of the consequences of behaviour. This type of learning was investigated by Thorndike (1911) during his studies of the problem-solving abilities of animals. Thorndike designed a puzzle box into which he would place a cat. The task for the cat inside the box was to escape. Inside the box there was a loop of string attached to a latch. When the string was pulled, the latch would lift and the door would open (see Diagram **B**).

Thorndike showed that a cat that was placed in a puzzle box would learn to pull a string to escape from the box. When it was first placed in the puzzle box, the cat moved around the box and by accident the string would be pulled and the latch would be lifted. This would happen each time the cat was placed in the box. However, after about 20 trials, Thorndike noticed that the cat began to escape very quickly. He suggested that the cat had learnt to escape from the box by trial and error learning. It was the pleasant consequence (escape) that encouraged the cat to pull the string rather than produce any other behaviours.

Key terms

Operant conditioning: learning due to the consequences of behaviour, through positive reinforcement or negative reinforcement.

Thorndike proposed a hypothesis:

If a certain response has pleasant consequences, it is more likely than other responses to occur in the same circumstances.

This became known as the **Law of Effect**.

B *Thorndike's apparatus*

Activity

2. You will need a bowl with 100 beads or counters in it. There should be five different colours and 20 of each colour. You need to choose one of the colours. Do this in your head, for example red. Place the bowl in front of a partner and tell them to pick out 50 beads. You will need an empty bowl for these beads to be placed in. Ask your partner to pick out a bead, then another and so on. As soon as they pick out a red one, nod and smile. Do this every time a red is chosen, but not for any other colour.

   When the 50 have been chosen, count how many of each colour there are. Are there more reds? There usually are. Why do you think this might happen?

Going further

There are lots of animals that are trained using operant conditioning. These include guide dogs and dogs that work for the police, bomb disposal and Customs. There are also animals that are trained to help people who are severely disabled.

Use the internet or other sources to investigate these animals and their training programmes. Make sure you note how operant conditioning plays a part in the training of these animals.

Did you know ??????

Many of the descriptions of animal training on these pages may seem to be concerned with getting animals to produce strange behaviours. However, there are some animals that can be trained to a very high level to produce some very *normal* behaviours. Capuchin monkeys are able to perform hundreds of actions to help a severely disabled person to live independently. These range from scratching an itch to opening the fridge, collecting a drink, putting it in a drink-holder and then adding a straw!

2 See if you can remember the terms that have been introduced in this topic so far. Write down each of the terms listed below. Then copy the correct definition alongside each one.

Terms	Definitions
Law of Effect	Learning that is due to consequences of behaviour, either rewards or **punishment**
Puzzle box	The rule that learning of a behaviour occurs when pleasant consequences follow that behaviour
Operant conditioning	A piece of apparatus used to study learning in animals

B F Skinner

Skinner (1938) introduced the idea of **reinforcement** to the Law of Effect. He said that all behaviour is learnt from the consequences of that behaviour. He called this *operant conditioning* because the animal or human produces a behaviour that is voluntary, so it 'operates' on the environment. The consequence of the particular behaviour produced by the animal or human will be to either increase or decrease the likelihood of the behaviour being repeated.

Much of Skinner's work involved his famous *Skinner box* (see Photo **C**). He would place a hungry rat in the box. The rat would produce a variety of actions such as sniffing, exploring and grooming. By accident it would press the lever and a pellet of food would immediately drop into the food tray. Every time the lever was pressed the behaviour of 'lever pressing' was positively reinforced by a food pellet.

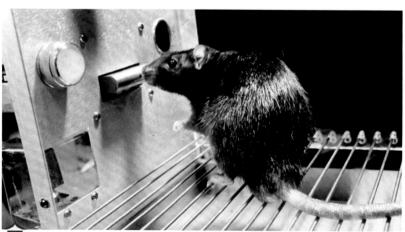

C A rat in the Skinner box

D B F Skinner

There are two kinds of reinforcement, **positive reinforcement** and **negative reinforcement**, but they have the same effect: to *increase* the likelihood that a particular behaviour will be repeated. Sometimes there would be an electric shock through the floor of the Skinner box. When the rat pressed the lever the shock would switch off. This is an example of negative reinforcement.

Punishment is quite different from reinforcement because it does not encourage the desired behaviour, it just stops one unwanted behaviour. A child, who is punished by having colouring pens taken away for writing on the wall, is very likely to find another object to scratch on the wall instead.

Reinforcement can be used to teach complex behaviours in animal and humans. This is called **behaviour shaping**. In this procedure the task is broken down into small steps. For a pigeon playing ping-pong, these steps might include moving towards the ball, touching the ball with its beak, hitting the ball, then hitting the ball towards another pigeon. The trainer reinforces the pigeon for moving towards the ball, so it will be given some grain for moving in the right direction towards the ball. Next, it will only get the grain when it has moved in the right direction *and* touched the ball. Over the conditioning trials the behaviour is shaped so that the whole sequence is produced for one reward at the end. Of course, to try this out you will need two pigeons!

E   *Pigeons playing ping-pong*

Activity

3   Parents often use positive reinforcement to encourage good behaviour. For example, if a parent wants a child to tidy their bedroom, they might offer money, 'If you tidy your room, I will give you £2'.

Can you see any implications of using positive reinforcement in this way? Discuss how it might be possible to use negative reinforcement to get the same child to tidy their bedroom. Remember, you will need to think of something unpleasant that will happen to the child until the correct response of 'tidying the room' occurs. Not too *unpleasant*!

Activity

4   a   Describe how behaviour shaping could be used to train a dog to fetch its lead. You will need to decide on each step of the whole procedure and on the reward you will use.

b   Think of examples where animals have their behaviour shaped in ways that mean they are essential to some people.

c   Can you think of any human behaviours that are or could be shaped in a similar way? Discuss this in small groups and exchange your ideas with other groups.

AQA *Examiner's tip*

Make sure that you are clear about the difference between negative reinforcement and punishment. Remember, punishment follows incorrect or unwanted behaviour; it does not strengthen or encourage the correct behaviour.

Check your understanding

1   Distinguish between 'reinforcement' and 'punishment'. *(3 marks)*

2   Explain what is meant by 'behaviour shaping'. *(3 marks)*

3   Describe how behaviour shaping could be used to encourage a child to eat using a knife and fork. *(4 marks)*

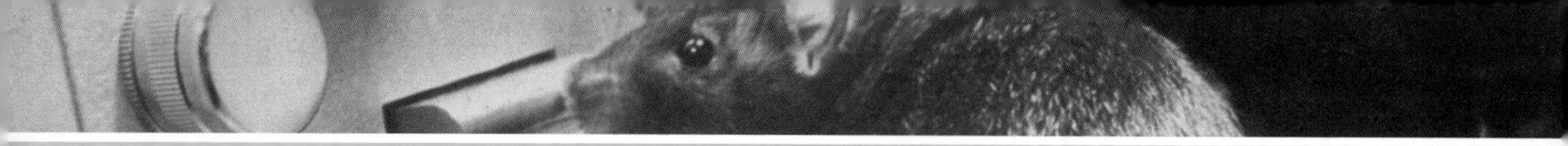

What are the applications of conditioning procedures?

Starter activity

1   As a group, conduct a fear survey to see what fears people have. Discuss whether or not these fears can be classed as **phobias**. If not, why not?

Conditioning procedures and phobias

We saw earlier that classical conditioning is concerned with the process of associating a new stimulus, like a bell, with a reflex response, like salivation. If we ring a bell and the dog salivates then we have built up new learning and established a conditional stimulus–conditional response (CS–CR) bond or connection. In order to understand how we might treat phobias, it is important to recognise that a phobia is a fear response that has gone wrong. The normal reflex is:

DANGER → FEAR

UCS   → UCR

When someone has a phobia, their fear response is to something that could cause or has little or no danger, such as:

KNEES → FEAR

CS   → CR

For the person with a phobia, their fear response is no longer the automatic response to a danger or threat. Instead it is to something that has little or no danger. This can be seen below in the common fear arachnophobia, the fear of spiders:

SPIDER → FEAR

CS   → CR

In order for the connection between the spider and fear to be made, the spider must have been present when something scary happened. One explanation for the fact that so many people develop a fear of spiders is that as young children we watch older people, such as brothers and sisters or mums and dads, very closely. If a person we admire, who normally takes care of us, suddenly screams and runs away when they see a spider, then we are exposed to the following sequence:

screaming makes me scared; spider + screaming makes me scared; spiders make me scared

You can see from Diagram **A** how a child might become afraid of balloons. Loud noises cause fear. When a child sees a balloon, which then pops, they are afraid because of the noise. Afterwards, just seeing a balloon causes fear. Understanding this connection has meant that psychologists have found ways of treating phobias.

Objectives

You will be able to:

describe and evaluate attempts to apply conditioning procedures to the treatment of phobias

understand the ethical implications of such attempts.

Key terms

Phobia: a persistent and irrational fear of an object, activity or situation. The typical symptoms are intense feelings of fear and anxiety to avoid the object, activity or situation.

Did you know ??????

There are over 530 names for different phobias that have been referred to in medical articles. Many websites list these names. Some are common fears, such as the fear of the number 13, triskaidekaphobia. Others are very unusual, like genuphobia, the fear of knees. The mental health organisation, Mind, has an excellent website with information for people who suffer from fears that affect their daily lives.

A *A classical conditioning schedule to show how a fear of balloons might be learnt*

Before conditioning – a reflex	Loud noise UCS	→	Fear UCR
During conditioning	Balloon + Loud noise CS UCS		Fear UCR
After conditioning	Balloon CS		Fear CR

Treatment of phobias

Flooding

In this treatment, the person is exposed repeatedly and rapidly to the thing they fear; they are flooded with thoughts and actual experiences. This means that someone with a fear of spiders would have to imagine a spider and perhaps visualise one running across the floor (thoughts) and then would have a spider in their hand (actual experience).

The way that flooding works is quite simple. The person has to unlearn the connection between the stimulus and the fear response: the CS–CR bond has to be broken. Most people with a phobia avoid or run away from the feared object. However, flooding prevents escape. Instead people learn that their anxiety levels start to drop the more times they are exposed to their fears. Flooding removes the phobia when a person realises they are not in danger and this happens quite quickly.

Ethical implications of flooding

Ethically there is a problem because the person loses their right to withdraw; for the treatment to work they have to stay. Also, it can be a very stressful procedure. This means that the psychologist has to judge exactly how much distress the person should undergo before stopping the treatment. It is difficult to protect and avoid harming someone who is being flooded.

links

To remind yourself of ethical considerations, see Topic 5.4.

Starter activity

2 For this activity you will need a partner. You need to measure the pulse rate of your partner so that you know how many beats per minute their normal pulse rate is. Then ask your partner to sit back, close their eyes and try to relax by thinking about a quiet, pleasant place. After two minutes measure their pulse rate again. Is there a difference in pulse rates between the normal and the relaxed states?

Systematic desensitisation

Systematic desensitisation as a treatment of phobias is based on the idea that people cannot be anxious and relaxed at the same time. As a person with a phobia cannot be afraid and relaxed at the same time, the fear response is replaced by feeling relaxed instead. The treatment works in the following way:

- The person with a phobia is taught how to relax themselves. This might involve listening to music and relaxing their muscles.

- The person and therapist construct a **hierarchy of fears** that contains the things they are afraid of in order from least frightening (the word 'spider') to most frightening (having a spider in my hand).

- The person relaxes and then gradually works through the hierarchy of fears, relaxing after each feared event is presented. The person only moves up the hierarchy if they have been relaxed at the previous stage. The final stage is to be relaxed at the 'most frightening' event.

Going further

There are many phobias and even different types of phobias. Research phobias on the internet. Produce a poster to show what you have found out. Make sure that the names and explanations of each phobia are clear and that the pictures are fun.

Picture of 'not real' spider   Picture of real spider

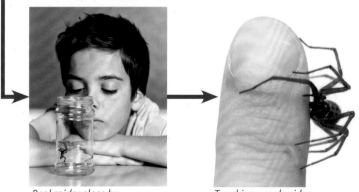

Real spider close by   Touching a real spider

B The stages of systematic desensitisation for the treatment of a fear of spiders

Practical applications

Treating a fear of balloons involves the following:

- The person is taught to relax, breathing deeply and calmly.
- The person constructs the hierarchy of fears in five stages:
  1 The word 'balloon'
  2 The squeaky sound of balloons being touched
  3 A picture of a balloon
  4 A real balloon
  5 Holding a balloon.
- The person is exposed to Stage 1 and must be completely relaxed while the word 'balloon' is repeated.
- The therapist then 'squeaks' a balloon out of sight of the person while the person relaxes.
- The therapist moves gradually through all the next stages until Stage 5 is achieved.
- There is no more fear of balloons, just a relaxed person!

C   *No more fear of balloons!*

Ethical implications

Systematic desensitisation is a treatment used when the therapist believes that flooding would be too stressful for the person with a phobia. Very often children are treated with this method. The therapist works with the person and together they decide on how quickly the person should move through the hierarchy. The person takes an active role in the therapy and can always withdraw from a stage if they feel uncomfortable. They can then practise relaxing again. There is no deception because the person knows exactly what is happening. As a result this is considered to be an ethical treatment for phobias.

Systematic desensitisation probably takes longer than flooding to remove a phobia but it is also an effective treatment. It can cost more as there are often more sessions of therapy. However, most therapists and their clients prefer this method of treatment. It is much less anxiety-arousing and much less stressful for the person undergoing treatment.

Activity

2   Working in small groups, choose a phobia that one group member has. List all their fearful situations and then construct a hierarchy of fears by getting them to rank the list. Each group could then present their hierarchy for discussion.

Check your understanding

1 What is a phobia? *(2 marks)*

2 Explain **one** ethical implication of using flooding to treat phobias. *(3 marks)*

3 Use your knowledge of systematic desensitisation to show how a child who is afraid of birds could be treated. *(4 marks)*

AQA   *Examiner's tip*

Remember not to confuse *application* and *implication*:

- One application of flooding is to treat phobias.
- One implication of flooding is that using it might mean treating people in an unethical way.

What are the other applications of conditioning procedures?

Starter activity

1 Copy the following classical conditioning schedule. Complete your table using the terms 'UCS' (unconditioned stimulus), 'UCR' (unconditioned response), 'CS' (conditioned stimulus) and 'CR' (conditioned response). One term has been done for you.

The completed schedule will demonstrate how a fear of cartoons might develop. In this case the dentist played cartoons while drilling his patient's teeth. Unfortunately, the final effect is not what the dentist might have expected.

Drilling teeth ⟶ Pain
UCS _____
Drilling teeth + Cartoon ⟶ Pain
_____ _____ _____
Cartoon ⟶ Pain
_____ _____

Objectives

You will be able to:

describe and evaluate aversion therapy

describe and evaluate token economy systems

understand the ethical implications of these methods.

Group activity

Divide into groups. Do you have any bad habits? These may not be really bad, but just behaviours you often wish you did not do, like biting your nails.

Choose **three** bad habits and discuss how classical conditioning might be used to unlearn each habit. For example, to stop someone biting their nails you could paint a horrible-tasting substance on the nails. Can you see how classical conditioning might explain why this would probably work?

A Smoking

B Nail biting

Aversion therapy

Another way that classical conditioning has been useful, is in the treatment of behaviour problems. Some therapists think that behaviour problems result from faulty learning and therefore that 'bad' behaviour can be unlearnt. A technique that has been used to help people who suffer from addictions like drug and alcohol dependency is called **aversion therapy**. The aim of the therapy is to get the patient to develop an extremely negative reaction to the drug or alcohol using the vomiting reflex. The procedure can be seen in Diagram **C**.

Key terms

Aversion therapy: a treatment for addictions, such as drug and alcohol dependency, which makes the addict have an extremely negative reaction to the addictive substance.

Emetic	→	Vomiting
UCS		UCR
Alcohol + Emetic	→	Vomiting
CS	UCS	UCR
Alcohol	→	Vomiting
CS		CR

C *Diagram showing how the classical conditioning procedure can be adapted to treat alcohol addiction (an emetic is a drug that causes immediate vomiting)*

This works because the emetic is specially designed so that it only produces the vomiting reflex when the patient drinks alcohol. (A simple everyday emetic could be very salty water. If you drink lots of that you will be sick and you will not be able to stop the vomiting.) The patient's desire for the alcohol decreases and the addiction can be overcome. Do not think that people who drink a lot are sick anyway so this treatment would not work. The emetic makes people sick immediately when they swallow the alcohol.

Although the therapy on its own can be successful, therapists believe that it is much more effective for aversion therapy to be used along with other support. This means helping the person to stay away from the situations where they used to spend time drinking. Also, aversion therapy can be a very unpleasant experience for the person and there are many ethical issues raised by this kind of treatment.

Did you know ??????

Autistic children sometimes produce very disturbing and self-harming behaviours such as repeated head-banging. Therapists have used aversion therapy to try to reduce this kind of behaviour. The head-banging is paired with an electric shock. The shock is painful enough to stop the child banging its head. Once this association is learnt, the child often does not revert to head-banging when the shocks stop. Of course, there are ethical implications in giving children electric shocks in this way.

Activity

1. Think about the possible outcomes of aversion therapy. Explain **one** positive evaluation point about the use of aversion therapy and **one** criticism of the procedure. Here you may want to consider the information on ethical issues in Topic 5.4.

Evaluation

Aversion therapy is used for some individuals who have serious behavioural problems. However, it can be extremely unpleasant for the person who has the treatment. Therefore the ethical issues of using this therapy have to be balanced against the possible benefits to the person. As you may find as a result of your research for the 'Going further' activity, aversion therapy is not always successful over time. Although people can find their addiction is reduced for a period, unless they have some additional support, they are likely to go back to their addictive behaviour once the treatment stops. This is particularly the case for younger addicts.

Going further

Find out how people who have suffered from alcoholism or drug dependency manage to keep themselves free from taking these substances. Use websites like Alcoholics Anonymous or Addiction Advisor for further information. You will probably notice that stopping taking the substance is only the first step. Staying substance-free is a difficult process that takes a long time to achieve. Discuss your findings with the rest of your group.

2 Think of all the rewards you have received over the last seven days. Make a table with two columns in it. Head the first column, 'Behaviour I produced' and the second column 'Reward I received'. Compare your list with a partner's list. Consider whether you would have produced the behaviour if there had not been a reward available. Think about why you might or might not have done so.

Token economy programmes

There are many things that can act as rewards or positive reinforcers. We know that food can encourage a rat to press a lever. Psychologists call a reinforcer like food a **primary reinforcer** because it is what the animal must have to survive. If a reinforcer can be exchanged for something then it is called a **secondary reinforcer**. For people, money is a secondary reinforcer because it can be exchanged for the things we need and those we want, like food, clothing, housing and holidays.

Token economy programmes have been set up in some hospitals, usually in psychiatric wards, to reward socially acceptable behaviour in people who may have stopped looking after themselves properly. Every time the person produces an appropriate behaviour, hospital staff *immediately* give the person a token. Tokens are given for making the bed, brushing teeth, and so on and can be used to 'pay for' activities like watching a favourite TV programme (this might 'cost' three tokens).

D *Prison programmes can improve behaviour*

Key terms

Primary reinforcer: a reward, such as food or water, that the animal or person needs in order to survive.

Secondary reinforcer: a reward, such as money or a token, that the animal or person can exchange for a primary reinforcer.

Did you know ??????

Token economy programmes have been used in prisons to encourage offenders to obey prison rules, complete tasks like their laundry, and to improve relationships with other prisoners and prison staff. When the offenders behave in positive ways, they are given tokens that can be exchanged for money and cigarettes. Studies have shown that behaviour in institutions where the system has been used has improved, at least inside the prison.

Evaluation

Token economies have produced improvements in the behaviour and self-care of patients who have been in hospital for a long time. However, they have been criticised by many people. Some critics argue that they make the patients focus on the reward rather than on wanting their own behaviour to improve. Even when the behaviour in hospital improves, this change might not last in the outside world. Remember too, if the reward is not immediate then the association between the reward and action is lost. This means that the behaviour is not being reinforced. There might also be ethical issues involved if patients are not able to watch a favourite TV programme because they have not got enough tokens.

There are many people who do not agree that behaviour should be manipulated or changed using systems like this, that rely on tokens. Some have suggested that, when we learn to produce good behaviour only because we receive a 'token/reward', we will not become social or kind humans. They have said that we need to learn to reward ourselves by *feeling good* when we do *good* things. We should not need other people to give us a reward all the time. Of course, praise can be an excellent reinforcer and, as we get older, we can feel good about ourselves for our good actions. In the same way we can feel guilty about our bad actions.

links

Here again, you need to consider the information on ethical issues in Topic 5.4.

Activity

2 Some schools use token economy systems to encourage good behaviour. These are often called merit or house point systems. Does your school have one of these? If so, does it work for all pupils? If you don't have a token economy system, would you like one? Explain why you think the benefits might or might not outweigh the problems. Discuss your thoughts with the rest of your group.

Check your understanding

1 A Year 7 form teacher has noticed that her pupils are not wearing the correct uniform. Describe how she might use a token economy system to improve the standard of dress in her form. *(4 marks)*

2 Outline **one** advantage of using a token economy system to clear litter in a school playground. Briefly discuss one problem of using a token economy system to clear the litter in the school playground. *(4 marks)*

3 Discuss practical implications of using aversion therapy and token economy systems to change unwanted behaviour. *(4 marks)*

AQA Examiner's tip

Remember, you should only write about the applications of conditioning techniques that are identified in the question that has been set. Writing about other possible treatments will not gain you marks. Also, *primary reinforcer* and *secondary reinforcer* are not terms that are named in the specification so you will not be asked to define them. You can, however, use them in an answer on token economy systems.

7 Social influence

7.1 What is conformity?

Starter activity

1 Make a list of five things you do with your friends or with your family. Ask yourself if you would do these things on your own if you had no one else to do them with. Who do you think has the most influence over what you do?

Why do we conform?

It has long been known that people's behaviour and even their opinions are influenced by others – this is called **social influence**. **Conformity** refers to the way in which our thoughts and actions are affected by the presence of those around us. Although we are sometimes aware of this happening, it can be an unconscious process. We do not necessarily realise just how much we change what we say or do because of others. Consciously, we may look to friends for guidance when we are unsure how to act. Unconsciously, we may copy the way they dress or even mirror their body language in certain situations.

Activity

1 Make a list of five ways in which you copy other people. Try to include some things that are good to copy as well as things that are bad.

The reasons why we copy others were explained by Deutsch and Gerrard (1955). Firstly, there is the need to be right. When we are in a situation that is 'ambiguous' (we are unsure of the correct thing to do or say) we will see what other people are doing and assume they are correct. This will lead us to copy them. This is especially the case if we believe others might have superior knowledge to ourselves. This might be due to their age or experience. For example, we might not know which fork to use in a restaurant, so we would see which one other people were using, then pick the same one.

Secondly, there is the need to be liked. When we are in a social situation, we have a strong desire to be accepted by the rest of the group. This means we are likely to do or say things that make us popular within that group. Of course, it is more important for us to be accepted by some people than by others. As a result, the extent to which our behaviour is affected will vary depending on whom we are with at the time. For example, we might go with our friends to see a film we don't really want to see because being with our friends is important to us.

Objectives

You will be able to:

understand what is meant by the term conformity

describe various factors that affect conformity

describe and evaluate studies of conformity.

Key terms

Social influence: the effect other people have on our behaviour. This includes conformity, obedience and social loafing, for example.

Conformity: a change in a person's behaviour or opinions as the result of group pressure.

⚭ links

See Topic 2.3 for information on postural echo (mirroring body language).

A *By watching others we may conform either consciously or unconsciously*

Did you know ???????

Research has shown that people with low self-esteem are more likely to conform than those with higher self-esteem.

Going further

Using the library or the internet, try to find the names Deutsch and Gerrard gave to these two different forms of social influence.

Sherif (1935)

Aim: To discover the effect on judgement of listening to other people.

Method: He asked participants to estimate how far a spot of light moved when they were sitting in an otherwise completely dark room. In fact the light didn't move at all, but owing to an optical illusion called the **autokinetic effect** it did appear to.

Results: Individually the participants gave a variety of estimates, which differed quite widely from each other's. However, after being allowed to undertake the same task in groups of three, their estimates became more similar until finally they were very close.

Conclusion: The participants used other people's opinions to help them form a judgement in an ambiguous situation.

Research study

Key terms

Autokinetic effect: an optical illusion, in which a spot of light on a screen appears to move, when in actual fact it doesn't.

AQA Examiner's tip

Remember to give an example when giving a definition in the exam, to help you explain what you mean.

Asch (1951) argued that Sherif's study was flawed precisely because the situation was ambiguous; the distance the light had moved was not known by the participants. So this did not demonstrate conformity.

Starter activity

2 Take a transparent container and fill it with coloured sweets, buttons or Lego bricks. Show it to a group of about 10 people at a time. Ask them each to secretly write down on small pieces of paper how many items they think are in the container. Gather the pieces of paper together and write each estimate in full view on a board or large piece of paper.

Now provide the group with an extra piece of information, such as the weight of the full container, and ask them to publicly call out a second estimate. See if the second estimates are any closer to each other than the first. You should find that they are.

Why do you think this is? Is it because of the extra information you provided, or is it because everyone heard what other people had said before they gave their second estimate?

Discuss why this should make a difference to the participants in your experiment.

B

Research study

Asch (1951)

Aim: Asch wanted to know whether people could be influenced by other people's opinions to give an answer they knew to be wrong. In this way it would be possible to see if people were conforming.

Method: Participants were shown sets of four lines. For each set, the participant had to say whether line A, B or C was the same length as the test line. When tested alone, the participants rarely made a mistake (the error rate was less than 1 per cent). However, participants also had to give their answers as part of a group. The rest of the group was instructed to give incorrect answers for some of the tests.

Results: On 32 per cent of the trials where the rest of the group gave the wrong answer, the participants gave the same wrong answer as the rest of the group, rather than the obviously correct answer. In fact 74 per cent of the participants gave at least one wrong answer.

Conclusion: The only reason for this 32 per cent error rate was hearing the incorrect answers previously given. Those who gave incorrect answers told Asch they knew their answers were wrong but did not want to go against the rest of the group. This clearly demonstrates normative social influence.

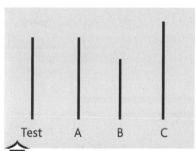

C *An example of the set of lines Asch showed to his participants*

D *A recreation of the Asch conformity experiment*

Evaluation

There are some problems with these pieces of research. Both of them were conducted in laboratories. This means that neither was a natural situation for the participants and so they may not have behaved in a natural way. As a consequence, the results might not be the same as they would be in an everyday situation. This is known as having 'low ecological validity'. Also, Asch carried out his research with university students, who may not behave in the same way as other people. This too could lead to inaccurate conclusions.

On the other hand, laboratory experiments offer a lot of control over the variables. When Asch conducted his research, he was able to alter several factors to see the impact on the rate of conformity. He found that if the task was more difficult, or there were more confederates giving incorrect answers, the rate of conformity increased. However, if the task was easier, or there was another person giving the correct answer, the rate went down.

∞ links

See pages 74–5 in Topic 5.1 for more information about the term 'ecological validity'.

Activity

2 In small groups, discuss the reasons why the difficulty of the task and the number of confederates affect the rate of conformity. Can you think of any other factors that might have an effect on this?

Something else to be considered when evaluating research into social influence is the use of confederates. If the participants are deliberately misled by people who are part of the research team, it is thought to be unethical. This is a criticism that applies throughout research in this topic.

Did you know ??????

Researchers in America found that over 97 per cent of juries stick with the initial decision of the majority. This shows the majority's power over people in the minority.

Check your understanding

1 Which one of the following two situations is an example of conformity because people want to fit in and be accepted by others?

   a Wearing the same style of clothes as your friends.

   b Answering a difficult question the same as someone else because you don't know the answer. *(1 mark)*

2 Describe **one** study in which conformity was investigated. Include in your answer the reason why the study was conducted, the method used, the results obtained and the conclusion drawn. *(4 marks)*

3 Identify and briefly describe **one** ethical issue that should be considered in conformity research. *(2 marks)*

AQA Examiner's tip

When you are asked to evaluate research, remember you could criticise problems with the method and discuss any ethical issues.

Starter activity

1   Make a list of the people whose orders we might follow if they told us what to do. Start from being young children, and finish with those whom we might obey when we are adults. Try to think why we obey them.

Why is it important to study obedience?

Obedience means following the orders of someone we perceive to be in a position of authority. Under normal circumstances this is perfectly acceptable because, for example, obeying parents or a police officer would keep us safe. However, history is littered with situations in which authority figures have given people unreasonable orders, with terrible consequences. Psychologists have tried to understand why we still obey, even when the orders we are given make us do things that we feel are wrong.

Activity

1   In a group, think of the ways in which obedience is different from conformity. To help you, think of whom we might obey, why we want to conform, and where and when we act like this.

Objectives

You will be able to:

understand what is meant by the term obedience

describe various factors that affect obedience

describe and evaluate studies of obedience.

Key terms

Obedience: following the orders of someone we believe to have authority.

Conformity: a change in a person's behaviour or opinions as the result of group pressure.

Research study

Milgram (1963)

Aim: Milgram wanted to see how far people would obey an unreasonable order.

Method: Forty male participants volunteered to take part in what they thought was an experiment about memory and learning. In this experiment they were made to believe they were giving an electric shock to a 'learner' every time he got an answer wrong. The learner was an actor and the shocks weren't real. However, the participant, who played the role of the teacher, didn't know this because of how convincing the experiment seemed. The participant was seated in front of a 'shock generator' that had 30 switches marked from 15 volts up to 450 volts.

The learner had to remember pairs of words, and the participant had to deliver a shock that increased in severity with each mistake the learner made. As the shocks increased, the participant heard the learner groan in pain, protest and eventually yell to be released. This was just a recording. After doing a lot of yelling, the learner then fell silent. This made the participant want to stop, so the experimenter would provide verbal prods such as, 'The experiment requires that you continue'.

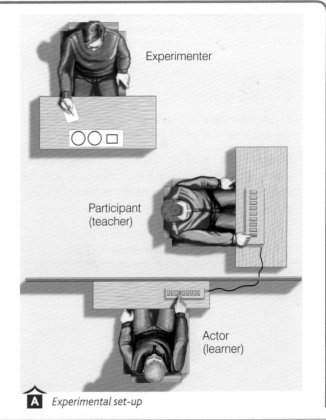

Experimenter

Participant (teacher)

Actor (learner)

A   *Experimental set-up*

15 – – – – –75 – – – – – 135 – – – – – 195 – – – – – 255 – – – – – 315 – – – – – 375 – – – – – 435   450
|VOLTS |30 |45 |60 |VOLTS |90 |105 |120 |VOLTS |150 |165 |180 |VOLTS |210 |225 |240 |VOLTS |270 |285 |300 |VOLTS |330 |345 |360 |VOLTS |390 |405 |420 |VOLTS |VOLTS |

| SLIGHT SHOCK | MODERATE SHOCK | STRONG SHOCK | VERY STRONG SHOCK | INTENSE SHOCK | EXTREME INTENSITY SHOCK | DANGER SEVERE SHOCK | X X X |

B   *The wording on the switches on the 'shock generator' in Milgram's experiment*

Results: Prior to the experiment, Milgram asked psychiatrists how far they thought the participants would go. The consensus was that no more than 1 per cent of them would deliver a 450 volt shock. However, despite the participants suffering a lot of distress (three of them actually had a seizure), they all delivered 300 volts, and 65 per cent of them went all the way to 450 volts.

Conclusion: People are prepared to obey quite extraordinary orders if they think the person giving them is in a position of authority.

Activity

2   What do you think of the Milgram study? Working with a partner, try to think of at least **two** criticisms (evaluations). Don't read on until you have attempted this activity.

Evaluation

It has been suggested that the participants realised that the shocks weren't real, which is why they went so far. However, their stress reactions and the fact that some of them did stop before the end makes this seem unlikely. The experiment has also been criticised for lacking ecological validity. However, it has been repeated in different situations with many variations and similar results have been found.

Activity

3   Milgram made many variations to his original procedure in order to see the impact on the participants.

Can you think of how the experiment could be changed to affect the results? What would make the obedience rate increase, and what would make it decrease? Think of things such as where the study took place, who was being shocked, who was giving the orders, the proximity of the experimenter and the learner, and any other things that might have an impact.

Put your conclusions into a display, and create a presentation for the rest of your group.

Did you know ??????

In a later study of obedience by Gamson (1982) participants refused to obey, and some even quoted Milgram's research as their reason. This shows that the experiment Milgram conducted has changed how people behave towards authority.

Starter activity

2 Can you think of reasons why people obey authority figures? Try to work out:

a Why do people obey in general?

b What specific things made Milgram's participants obey in his experiment?

Share your ideas with the rest of your group.

■ Further studies

Several other studies of obedience have taken place in more everyday situations.

C *A mother tells her son how to behave near a busy road and hopes he will obey*

Research study

Hofling *et al.* (1966)

Aim: To see if people would follow an unreasonable order in their normal work environment.

Method: Hofling contacted 22 nurses individually by phone. Claiming to be a doctor, he instructed them to give a patient twice the maximum dosage of a drug called 'Astrofen'.

Results: Of the 22, 21 were prepared to follow his orders, despite the maximum dosage being clearly marked on the bottle.

Conclusion: Nurses are likely to obey the instructions of a doctor even when there may be bad consequences for a patient.

Bickman (1974) created a simple field experiment to investigate the effect of the way someone giving an order is dressed.

Research study

Bickman (1974)

Aim: He wanted to know if people would be more likely to obey an order if it came from someone in a uniform.

Method: He had actors dress as either a security guard or just in a casual jacket. They each asked people sitting in a park to pick up some litter.

Results: What he found was that 80 per cent of people obeyed the 'guard' compared with 40 per cent when the actor wasn't wearing a uniform.

Conclusion: Wearing a uniform will increase the sense that a person is a legitimate authority figure.

Evaluation

Although Bickman's study has a lot more ecological validity, owing to its being conducted beyond a laboratory setting, the same cannot be said of Hofling's experiment. The drug used was not a real drug, and the nurses weren't allowed to discuss the request with anyone. This made the study less realistic, despite the apparent normality of the situation.

Activity

4 What all of these studies seem to show is that obedience is a bad thing. However, it isn't always.

Divide into two groups and consider reasons why obedience is a bad thing and why it is a good thing. Each group should consider one of these aspects. Present your findings to the other group. Have an independent person, such as your teacher or lecturer, judge which group produces the better arguments.

Activity

5 What do you think of these last two studies? Do you think they are likely to be more or less reliable than the Milgram study? Why?

AQA *Examiner's tip*

Remember that each of these pieces of research is unethical because they both involve deception and a lack of informed consent.

Reasons for obedience

A number of reasons for obedience have been identified:

- **Socialisation** – throughout our lives, and especially when we are young, we are taught to obey authority figures, such as parents and teachers. This means that it becomes a normal thing for us to do.

- Legitimate authority – the experimenter wearing a lab coat and the prestige of Yale University (where the Milgram study was conducted) made the participants put faith in the person telling them what to do. In a similar way, we might unquestioningly obey a doctor because we have faith in their superior knowledge.

- Gradual commitment – as the shocks in Milgram's study started quite low and increased by such small steps, it was difficult for the participants to know where to draw the line. After all, if you have given someone a shock of 150 volts already, why not 165 volts?

- **Buffers** – as the participants could not directly see the victim of their actions, they were shielded from the consequences of what they did. This made it easier for them to deal with.

- Not feeling responsible – Milgram suggested that the situation he had created caused people to lose their sense of responsibility for their own actions. Normally, we feel responsible for what we do. However, here the participants were acting on behalf of someone else; they were just doing as they were told. This stopped them from feeling they would be blamed for what they did.

Key terms

Socialisation: the way we are raised to behave and the things we are taught to accept as normal.

Buffer: something that creates distance between the teacher and learner (e.g. a wall or another person administering the shocks).

∞ links

Deindividuation has also been shown to be a factor affecting obedience. For an explanation of what this means, see Topic 7.3.

Going further

Milgram's research has been repeated in different countries, with both men and women. See if you can find whether these results were similar to or different from his original results.

Check your understanding

1 Identify and explain **one** factor that affects obedience. Refer to psychological research in your answer. *(4 marks)*

2 Read each of the following statements and decide whether **it is true or false**:

   a   We are more likely to obey someone in a position of authority than a friend. *(1 mark)*

   b   Obedience studies are all conducted in an ethical way. *(1 mark)*

   c   Wearing a uniform makes a person more likely to be obeyed. *(1 mark)*

3 Describe **one** study in which obedience was investigated. Include in your answer the reason why the study was conducted, the method used, the results obtained and the conclusion drawn. *(4 marks)*

AQA Examiner's tip

Remember, when describing a study, you must include all the parts that have been asked for. If you miss out any one part, you cannot get full marks, even if the rest are very well described.

Starter activity

1 Think of **three** things you might do if you were in a group that you wouldn't do if you were alone. Can you think why people act differently when others are around?

Activity

1 Conduct a survey. Ask people if they could be a superhero, what super power they would choose to have. Provide them with a list of alternatives, such as being able to fly or being very strong. You can include any powers you like but make sure you include being able to become invisible. If people are invisible, no one will know it is they who are doing anything and there will be very few restraints on their behaviour. This is the same as **deindividuation**.

Survey

If you could be a superhero, what super power would you choose to have?

- Super strength
- Ability to fly
.
.
.

Objectives

You will be able to:

understand what is meant by the term deindividuation

describe various factors that affect deindividuation

describe and evaluate studies of deindividuation.

■ How does deindividuation happen?

It was Festinger (1952) who first used the term 'deindividuation' to refer to what happens when people lose their sense of individuality. Individuality refers to who we are: our personality, our values, our conscience, and so on. An important part of this is our sense of right and wrong – when deindividuation occurs people lose this. A consequence is that people lose their sense of responsibility for what they do and stop being able to judge whether their actions are right or wrong.

Most people behave in socially acceptable ways because if they didn't there would be the threat of punishment for them. However, a person can only be punished if it is clear who is responsible for any wrongdoing. Festinger suggested that deindividuation is most likely to occur when we are in a crowd because we become **anonymous**. This means that, if a person behaves like everyone else in the group, he or she cannot be identified as an individual. Once you join a group, your identity becomes harder to distinguish and so the threat of punishment for anything you do decreases. If no one knows who you are, you can't be punished for anything you do. This is one reason why deindividuation leads to antisocial behaviour. It is why mobs behave very differently from people on their own.

Deindividuation was investigated by Zimbardo (1969) with a field experiment conducted in New York and a small town in California called Palo Alto. He thought big cities were anonymous places and he wanted to see the effect this would have on behaviour.

Key terms

Deindividuation: the state of losing our sense of individuality and becoming less aware of our own responsibility for our actions.

Anonymous: being able to keep our identity hidden.

⬭links

See Topic 9.1, which deals with the causes of aggression, and Topic 9.2, which discusses studies of aggression.

Research study

Zimbardo (1969)

Aim: To see if people in a big city behave in a more antisocial way than people in a small town.

Method: He parked a car in each place with its bonnet up, as if it had broken down, and observed what people did as they passed by.

Results: Immediately people began stealing parts off the car in New York, and within two weeks there was very little of it left. In Palo Alto, the only time the car was touched was when someone lowered the bonnet to stop the engine getting wet when it was raining.

Conclusion: The deindividuation caused by living in a big city leads to an increase in antisocial behaviour.

A *City versus small town*

The second of Zimbardo's studies was designed to investigate the effect of adding a variable to Milgram's original procedure.

Zimbardo (1969)

Aim: To see the effect of hiding the identity of participants on the size of electric shock they are prepared to give someone.

Method: Female university students were put into one of two groups when playing the role of the teacher. The first group had to wear laboratory coats with hoods to hide their faces and they weren't introduced to each other. The second group wore their own clothes and name badges.

Results: The shocks given by the first group were twice as great as the shocks given by the second group.

Conclusion: Being able to hide their identity leads people to behave in crueller ways than they otherwise would because the person on the receiving end does not know who they are. This means there are less likely to be any consequences for what they do.

Evaluation

- This study lacked **mundane realism**. This means the participants might not behave how they normally would.
- This study raised several ethical issues, such as deception and psychological harm.

links

Refresh your memory of Milgram's study before you read about Zimbardo's second study. Look back to Topic 7.2 on page 104.

Did you know ??????

Perhaps Zimbardo's most famous study involved using students to play the roles of prisoners and guards in a mock prison at Stanford University. Despite it being a role-play situation, the students quickly came to behave like prisoners and guards, and the study had to be stopped due to the harm that the 'prisoners' were experiencing.

Activity

2   In groups of three or four, consider the strengths and weaknesses of the previous two studies by Zimbardo. Evaluate his methods and his conclusions. Could there be other reasons for his findings than deindividuation? Were his studies ethical?

Present your conclusions to your whole group.

Key terms

Mundane realism: an everyday situation, that is life-like and not artificial.

2 Plan a study to investigate deindividuation. Consider where you would carry out the study. Would you use a field experiment or an observation? Finally, ask yourselves if it is possible to do this without breaking any ethical guidelines.

Factors affecting deindividuation

Being able to hide one's identity

Zimbardo's second study didn't place the participants in groups but he was able to conceal their identities in other ways and so maintain their anonymity. This again was able to remove the threat of punishment.

However, deindividuation isn't just about removing the threat of punishment. It is also about losing a sense of your own identity, and this can happen in several ways.

Wearing a uniform

We are often encouraged to behave like other people by the roles we have to play. We wear uniforms to make us like everyone else and there are accepted norms for us all. When we belong to a group, we are expected to behave like the others in that group. There may even be written guidelines or 'codes of conduct' for us to have to follow. In such cases, we don't make our own decisions on how to behave. We are discouraged from being individuals. For example, when we meet a doctor or a policeman, we want them to be just the same as any other doctor or policeman. We expect them to all play the same roles, and not be individuals.

Being part of a gang or clearly identifiable group

Sometimes the uniforms we wear are informal, and yet other people still see us as belonging to a group. People then expect us to behave like others in that group. For example, if we dress like a goth or a football supporter, people expect us to behave like a goth or a football supporter. Deindividuation occurs when we behave like the group we are in rather than like an individual.

Closed-circuit television (CCTV): a television system often used for surveillance.

Research has shown how anonymity affects people's behaviour in real life. When crowds gather to watch someone threatening to commit suicide by jumping off a building, the more anonymous people can be (the crowd is large, it is dark, or they are a long way from the jumper), the more likely they are to encourage the person to do it (Mann, 1981).

B

∞ **links**

See Topic 4.1 for information on stereotyping.

C *Graffiti often appears where there is a wall that is hidden from view*

D *People are more likely to engage in antisocial behaviour when they are in a large crowd or a gang*

It has been found that when people are in crowds, they adopt the mood of that crowd and change their behaviour accordingly. So if the crowd is happy (e.g. a carnival atmosphere), people joining it will also become happy. If on the other hand it is an angry mob, the people will become angry. Once again, we are not behaving like an individual, but rather as part of a group.

Practical applications

A practical application of research into deindividuation is to prevent situations in which people can remain anonymous. CCTV cameras are being used increasingly to monitor people's behaviour in shopping centres and car parks. Psychologists would agree that being able to identify individuals in a crowd would help reduce antisocial behaviour. If people know they can be identified, they are less likely to engage in aggressive behaviour, theft or vandalism.

Practical implications

An implication of research into deindividuation is that, when people are wearing uniforms in the workplace, they do not behave like individuals, but as members of a business or firm. People are made to wear uniforms so that they are easily identifiable and are less likely to try to be different from others in their company. This is one reason why children are required to wear school uniforms. It makes it harder for them to act independently, and so easier to be controlled by a set of rules that apply to everyone.

Activity

4   Imagine you have been asked by the government to conduct research into whether having to carry identity cards is a good thing or a bad thing.

Before you carry out a survey to ask people's opinions, you must present your own thoughts about it. In small groups, create a table with arguments for and against use of identity cards. Remember what studies of deindividuation have shown us.

Present your conclusions to the whole group, and put your table on the wall for everyone to read.

Check your understanding

1   Read each of the following statements and decide whether each is true or **false**:

a   Anonymity will have no effect on deindividuation. *(1 mark)*

b   Deindividuation increases self-awareness. *(1 mark)*

2   Describe **one** study in which deindividuation was investigated. Include in your answer the reason why the study was conducted, the method used, the results obtained and the conclusions drawn. *(4 marks)*

Activity

3   Using what you have learned about deindividuation in this topic, discuss how wearing hoods affects how people behave. Think of things like graffiti, vandalism and violence. What suggestions might psychologists make to help reduce the effects of deindividuation?

AQA   *Examiner's tip*

Remember, when you evaluate Zimbardo's studies, one of them was based in a laboratory, which is not a normal situation for the participants. However, the other one was a field experiment, so he was measuring realistic behaviour.

Going further

One aspect of deindividuation is the way it enables people to do and say things that they wouldn't do and say if they could be recognised and their identities were known. They feel they can get away with things they wouldn't in a face-to-face situation. Because of this, online dating has had both successes and problems.

Consider the reasons why some people might prefer to use online dating. Consider also the dangers that these people face when they do. Create a presentation for the rest of your group to explain your conclusions.

Starter activity

Try to think of three things you do that you don't put as much effort into when you are in a group as you do when you are on your own. An example could be when singing in a choir compared with when singing on your own.

Studies of social loafing

Around a hundred years ago it was discovered that when people are in groups, they do not put in as much effort as people doing the same task on their own. This became known as **social loafing**. It was found during a tug-of-war that the more men there were pulling the rope, the less effort they each put in. For example, five people should be able to apply five times the force that one person can, but this doesn't happen. When a group of people are all performing a task together, every person is being helped by others. As a result it is not possible to identify an individual person's performance. This means they do not need to work as hard as they do on their own.

Activity

1   You each need an A3 sheet of plain paper with a series of small boxes on it. (Create one sheet and then photocopy for the whole group.) How long does it take one person alone to colour in all the boxes?

For the second part of the experiment, four people need to work together on an identical sheet of paper colouring in the boxes. How long does it take them?

It should take them a quarter of the time to complete the task that one person took. If social loafing has occurred, it will take them longer than this, because they are not putting in as much effort.

Research study

Latané *et al*. (1979)

Aim: To see whether being in a group would have an effect on how much effort participants put into a task.

Method: Researchers asked 84 participants to shout and clap as loudly as they could while they were alone or in groups of up to six. Each participant wore headphones so they couldn't hear the others.

Results: The larger the group size, the less noise the participants made.

Conclusion: People put less effort into doing something when they know others are contributing effort to the same task than they do when they are the only one.

Objectives

You will be able to:

understand what is meant by the term social loafing

describe various factors that affect social loafing

describe and evaluate studies of social loafing.

Key terms

Social loafing: putting less effort into doing something when you are with others doing the same thing.

Culture: a group of people (usually living in one place) who share similar customs, beliefs and behaviour.

A   *In a tug-of-war, a person doesn't pull as hard when there are more people pulling*

Did you know ??????

This is also known as the Ringelmann effect, after Max Ringelmann, who conducted the tug-of-war study.

Earley (1989)

Aim: To see if **culture** makes a difference to social loafing.

Method: Participants from the US and China had to complete tasks alone and in groups. The level of social loafing was measured by how much effort was put in to the task in each condition by the participants.

Results: The American participants reduced the amount of effort they put in to the task when they were in groups, but the Chinese did not.

Conclusion: Social loafing does not exist in all cultures. In some cultures people are prepared to work just as hard for the good of the whole group even when they do not need to.

Evaluation

All the people in the Latané study were from the same culture. In some cultures, people are more concerned with the welfare of their group rather than with merely looking out for themselves. This means that they value their family, their work colleagues or even their country more highly than their own needs, and social loafing might not occur.

In the Earley study only two countries were compared. People who live in Africa for instance might behave differently again.

Activity

3   Do you think the type of activity you are doing will affect whether social loafing occurs? In groups of four, make a list of four activities that you do with other people (each of you suggest one activity). Try to work out what factors will make social loafing more or less likely to happen.

How will you make sure everyone contributes to this activity? Don't read on until you have attempted this activity.

Factors that affect social loafing

There are various factors that affect social loafing:

- the size of the group you are with
- the nature of the task you are performing
- the culture to which you belong.

Check your understanding

1   What is meant by the term 'social loafing'? *(2 marks)*

2   Describe **one** study in which social loafing was investigated. Include the reason why the study was conducted, the method used, the results obtained and the conclusion drawn. *(4 marks)*

3   Read each of the following statements and decide whether it is *true* or *false*:

a   The number of people in a group will affect the amount of effort each person puts into a task. *(1 mark)*

b   Culture has no effect on social loafing. *(1 mark)*

Activity

2   What do you think of the studies of social loafing that have been described? Working with a partner, try to think of **two** evaluations of each piece of research.

Going further

Apart from social loafing, there are other areas of research in which culture has an effect on behaviour. Can you find any other research described in this book that might be affected by cultural differences?

AQA Examiner's tip

Remember, when you are evaluating a piece of research, it is possible to make the comment that the findings would not always be the same in every culture. This demonstrates that you are thinking beyond the study.

What is bystander intervention?

7.5 omould 38%

1 Imagine someone has dropped a bag of shopping as you are walking past. You may decide to stop and help pick up the spilt contents, or you may not. Make two columns on a piece of paper: in the first column write down reasons why you would help and in the second write down reasons why you would not help.

Objectives

You will be able to:

understand what is meant by the term 'bystander intervention'

describe various factors that affect bystander intervention

describe and evaluate studies of bystander intervention.

Case study

Kitty Genovese

In 1964, a young woman named Kitty Genovese was attacked in New York. She was only yards from her home, and the attack continued for over half an hour before she was eventually killed. Only afterwards did someone call the police, who arrived within four minutes. When the neighbours were questioned, 38 of them were able to say what had happened and to give a description of the murderer. This means that any one of them could have prevented the murder by calling the police straight away instead of just watching. Yet no one did.

Activity

1 In groups, discuss why you think people did not do anything when Kitty Genovese shouted for help. It has been suggested that, when living in a big city, it is safer to mind your own business than get involved with people you don't know. Apart from the threat to personal safety, do you think there are other reasons why people did nothing to help?

Latané and Darley (1968) believed the reason people do not offer help in such situations is because of the presence of other people around them. So to investigate this, they set up an investigation in a laboratory.

Research study

Latané and Darley (1968)

Aim: To see if people are less likely to react in an emergency when there are others present.

Method: They had participants sit in a room either alone or in threes while completing a questionnaire. While the participants were doing this, smoke began pouring into the room.

Results: Of the participants, 75 per cent of those sitting alone went to tell someone about the smoke within six minutes, whereas only 38 per cent of those in groups of three did.

Conclusion: If there are other people around you, it will make it less likely that you will react in an emergency.

A *The more people there are present, the less likely they are to offer help to someone who needs it*

Evaluation

You need to remember that this study was conducted in a laboratory. In an everyday situation people might behave differently.

One of the reasons for the results in the study is **diffusion of responsibility**. When you are alone in an emergency situation, you have to act because there is no one else around to offer any help. However, when there are others present, you can let someone else do it. In the case of Kitty Genovese, no one knew whether anyone else had already phoned the police. It may have seemed likely that someone had, and that thought would have prevented people from phoning the police.

Sometimes it is hard to determine whether or not a situation is in fact an emergency. When children scream for instance, it might be that they are playing rather than they have hurt themselves. So sometimes the only way to know whether an emergency is happening is to look at the reactions of other people. Once again, when there are others present this might hinder helping behaviour because they might not know whether it is an emergency either. When you see other people who aren't reacting, it makes you think the situation definitely isn't an emergency.

> **Key terms**
>
> **Diffusion of responsibility:** in a group of people there is less need for the individual to act because someone else who is present could also do something.

Going further

1 Ecological validity is mentioned a lot in psychological research but this doesn't only apply to laboratories. Can you think of any reasons why case studies or experiments conducted in New York might provide different results to research done elsewhere?

Angel Torres

Angel Torres, 78, remains paralyzed below the neck and in critical condition at Hartford Hospital. He was crossing Park Street when he was hit by a car. The driver of the car didn't stop, but it's what happens next that is so upsetting.

Nothing!

The traffic camera shows 10 cars pass Torres lying on the ground. Two others turn around and go the opposite way. The police said four people did call 9-1-1, but no one on the sidewalk immediately rushed over to see how he was. Torres was lying in the street for nearly a minute and a half before a police cruiser on its way to another call found him lying there.

Channel 8 News, 6 June 2008

Activity

2 Read the extract about Angel Torres.

In groups, can you think of reasons why no one helped Angel Torres? Is it just because there were other people around, or are there other reasons? How do you think you would have reacted if you had witnessed this event?

Further studies of bystander behaviour

Further research in this area has investigated different factors that might affect bystanders' behaviour.

B Would you stop to help?

Research study

Piliavin (1972)

Aim: To see if the appearance of the victim would influence helping behaviour.

Method: Piliavin had an actor pretend to collapse in a train carriage. His appearance was altered several times and the amount of help he received each time was recorded by an observer.

Results: When the 'victim' carried a walking stick, he received help within 70 seconds, 90 per cent of the time. When he had an ugly facial scar, this dropped to 60 per cent. When he appeared to be drunk, it dropped to 20 per cent.

Conclusion: The appearance of the person needing help will affect whether and how quickly they get that help.

Evaluation

You need to ask yourself what other factors could have affected the results in this study. In a train carriage there are lots of variables that the researcher cannot control.

In 1983, Bateson conducted an experiment to show how the characteristics of a victim can have a different sort of impact on whether they receive help or not.

Research study

Bateson *et al.* (1983)

Aim: To discover if the similarity of a victim to the bystander will affect whether or not they receive help.

Method: Participants watched a woman who they thought was receiving electric shocks. Each participant was made to think the woman was either like themselves or not like themselves. They were then given the opportunity to take the woman's place in order to stop her suffering.

Results: More participants were prepared to take the place of the woman they thought to be similar to themselves than dissimilar.

Conclusion: People are more likely to offer help to someone they feel is similar to themselves in some way than to someone they cannot relate to. Bateson claimed it is because we feel greater **empathy** for people like ourselves, and it causes us more distress to see them suffering. Helping them relieves this distress.

One way of analysing whether people will help others is to understand the costs and rewards involved in helping. When faced by a situation that requires some sort of action, people assess what it will cost them to help and what kind of reward they might expect to gain. If they decide that the costs are higher than the rewards, they might decide to do nothing. **Altruism** occurs when bystanders do not consider the costs at all but help people purely because they need help. This is a highly debated aspect of human behaviour. Some psychologists believe altruism does not exist and that those who help in an emergency have just made a decision to do so after considering the costs and rewards.

Latané and Darley referred to the situation when people do nothing to help in an emergency as **bystander apathy**. However, Schroeder *et al.* (1995) thought 'apathy' was not the right term to use, and re-examined the data from several pieces of research.

Schroeder *et al.* (1995)

Aim: To explore different reasons for bystanders not helping.

Method: They studied the findings and conclusions from many previous pieces of research.

Results: They were able to provide an alternative explanation for why bystanders did nothing to help when others were present.

Conclusion: Bystanders are distressed and concerned about victims but, when other people are present, they believe that someone else might be more capable of helping, or can help more easily than themselves.

Research study

Going further

2   There have been many studies conducted to investigate bystander intervention. Using the library or internet, try to find another study in this area. Note down the reason why the study was conducted, the method used, the results gained and the conclusion drawn. Also include any evaluation you feel is appropriate. Put your findings on a large piece of paper that may be displayed on the wall or presented to your group.

Check your understanding

1   Read each of the following statements and decide whether it is **true** or **false**:

   a   Bystanders are more likely to offer help in an emergency if there are more people there. *(1 mark)*

   b   Bateson found bystanders are more likely to help those who are similar to them than those who are dissimilar. *(1 mark)*

   c   Bystander apathy occurs when people do nothing to help in an emergency. *(1 mark)*

2   Identify **two** factors affecting bystander intervention. *(2 marks)*

3   Describe **one** study that has been conducted by Latané and Darley to investigate bystander intervention. Include in your answer the reason why the study was conducted, the method used, the results gained and the conclusion drawn. *(4 marks)*

Group activity

2   In groups, draw up a chart with three columns. In the first column write situations in which you might help someone, for example holding a door open for them. In the second column, write down what it will cost you. And in the third column, write down what you might gain from it. Try to think of psychological rewards, such as feeling good about yourself, as well as physical rewards, such as money. Present your grid to the rest of the group.

Activity

3   Make a list of the factors that affect bystander intervention.

AQA Examiner's tip

Remember, when evaluating a piece of research, it is sometimes possible to interpret the results in more than one way, and so reach different conclusions.

Behaviour outside a laboratory

Objectives

You will be able to:

understand the practical implications of studies of social influence.

Starter activity

Look at the following names of psychologists, and try to match them up with a description of their studies of bystander intervention. See if you can do it without the help of your book first of all. If you have difficulty, use your book to refresh your memory.

	Psychologist(s)		Description of study
1	Bateson	A	Filled a room with smoke to see if people alone would react quicker than when they are in groups of three
2	Piliavin	B	Analysed previous research and concluded that bystanders might not help because they think others might be more qualified
3	Latané and Darley	C	Manipulated the appearance of an actor falling over on the New York subway to see how it affected helping behaviour
4	Schroeder	D	Tested the effect of the 'victim's' similarity on helping behaviour

Key terms

Practical implications: suggestions about behaviour in the real world beyond the research study, based upon what psychologists have discovered.

AQA Examiner's tip

Remember, when you are asked to provide **practical implications** of research, you need to think what it tells us about behaviour in the real world, away from the research laboratory.

Activity

1   Can you think of realistic situations in which people conform?

Psychologists have implied that conformity is a bad thing. Next to each example you think of, say whether conformity is a good thing or a bad thing.

Share your opinions with the rest of your group.

Implications of research into conformity

Studies of conformity have shown that it is hard for individuals to act differently from the rest of the group. One occasion when the implications of this might be quite serious is in the decision-making process of a jury. It is highly likely that if 11 people in a jury believe the defendant to be guilty, the final juror will agree with them even if privately he or she believes otherwise. This is because of the difficulty of having to disagree with a majority.

Did you know ? ? ? ? ?

All the research discussed in this chapter suggests that the way people behave is determined by the situations in which they find themselves. These causes are known as 'situational factors'. If the behaviour is caused by internal factors, such as their personalities, the causes are known as 'dispositional factors'.

A   *A group of children conforming in the way they are dressed and the way they are sitting*

Implications of research into obedience

Milgram's research has been able to provide an explanation for why the space shuttle *Challenger* was allowed to explode when it could have been prevented. It has been well documented that some engineers anticipated the breakage of the part that caused the explosion before the launch, but they were persuaded to say nothing by the authority figures within their organisation. Through his research, Milgram showed that it is easy to do as you are told and quite hard to disobey in such a situation.

Implications of research into social loafing

Social loafing has shown us that when people belong to a group they reduce the amount of effort they put into a task. This is because it is not possible to identify an individual's performance. This means that some people will be trying harder than others, and no one can tell who these people are. This may occur when playing team games. Unlike tennis or golf, where an individual competes alone, in hockey or rugby, some players may not do as much running or tackling as others. We can also make predictions about the behaviour of students, based on the research in this area. When students are given presentations to prepare for in groups, some will do most of the work while others will be able to get away with making very little contribution to the group at all.

Implications of research into bystander intervention

In 1993, two-year-old James Bulger was abducted, by two boys, from a shopping centre in Bootle. They took him to some waste ground and murdered him. What has research into bystander intervention led us to believe bystanders would do if they witnessed the abduction? Nothing! Research has shown us that people, who witness a small boy being dragged through the streets crying for his mother, are unlikely to intervene. Latané and Darley showed that, when lots of people are around, it reduces the chance of someone helping. It is hard to realise that there is an emergency when other people are doing nothing. Even if anyone did realise, diffusion of responsibility would stop people from getting involved. This is indeed what happened to James Bulger – no one helped.

Activity

2   Milgram's research has provided an explanation for why the Jews were treated so badly by Nazi soldiers in Germany. He showed that ordinary people would follow unreasonable orders if they were given by an authority figure.

In groups, discuss whether or not you think the general public should be made aware of Milgram's research. Do you think it was a good piece of research, or not?

⬤⬤ **links**

See page 111 in Topic 7.3 for the practical implications of research into deindividuation.

Going further

Using newspapers or the internet, see if you can find any real-life situations that demonstrate deindividuation. Do these situations demonstrate what psychologists have found about the way people behave? Print any articles you find and put them on the classroom wall.

Check your understanding

1   Use your knowledge of psychology to explain **one** practical implication of studies of deindividuation. *(3 marks)*

2   Read each of the following statements and decide if it is **true** or **false**:

   a   Studies of social loafing have shown that people work harder in groups than they do alone. *(1 mark)*

   b   Research into bystander intervention shows that the appearance of a 'victim' will affect the amount of help she receives. *(1 mark)*

   c   Studies of obedience have shown that people are more likely to obey someone who is wearing a uniform than someone who is not. *(1 mark)*

8 Sex and gender

8.1 What is the distinction between sex identity and gender identity?

■ Sex identity and gender identity

Sex is a biological term. A child is either male or female. The sex identity of a child can be identified at birth by biological factors such as hormones and chromosomes:

- The male hormone is known as testosterone.
- The female hormone is known as oestrogen.
- The male sex chromosomes are XY.
- The female sex chromosomes are XX.

Gender is a psychological term. It refers to ideas about the expected attitudes and behaviour of males and females in a particular culture. The gender identity of a child can be identified from the way they act, dress and speak.

For most people, there is a match between their sex identity and their gender identity. For example, there is a match between sex identity and gender identity when a boy thinks and behaves in a masculine way. This, however, is not always the case. There may be boys who think and behave in a feminine way.

One distinction between sex identity and gender identity is that sex identity is defined in the same way in all cultures whereas gender identity can be different in different cultures. For example, in Britain we distinguish between two different gender identities: masculine and feminine. The Mohave Indians, however, recognise four different gender identities: traditional males, traditional females, males who choose to live as women and women who choose to live as men.

Girls might show feminine gender behaviour by, for example, wearing pink clothes and playing with dolls. Boys might show masculine gender behaviour by playing football and being aggressive.

A *Masculine gender identity*

∞ links

See Topic 9.1 for definitions of hormones and chromosomes.

Activities

1   Identify any other differences you can think of between the terms 'sex identity' and 'gender identity'.

2   Working in pairs:

a   Identify ways that a five-year-old girl would show a feminine gender identity.

b   Identify ways that a five-year-old boy would show a masculine gender identity.

B   *Feminine gender identity*

Boys will be boys?

Mothers say that bringing up boys is very different to bringing up girls. One mother stated that while her daughter likes singing and playing with dolls, her sons enjoy rough and tumble play and getting dirty. When they get home from school they like to play football or cricket in the garden. She says that the house is never tidy while they're around because they leave their toys and clothes wherever they go. Her husband tells her not to try and change them because that is what boys are like.

Case study

C

Did you know ??????

Gender Identity Disorder describes people who have strong feelings of being born with the wrong gender.

Activity

3   Read the case study and answer the following questions:

a   Identify **three** ways that the boys are showing masculine behaviour.

b   Explain how the comment made by their father shows that the gender behaviour the boys are showing is society's expected way for them to behave.

Going further

1   Interview a parent about the gender behaviour of his or her child. Remember to consider ethical issues when preparing and asking your questions.

Ask the parent questions including:

a   At what age did your child begin to show masculine or feminine behaviour?

b   Give some examples of the masculine or feminine behaviour your child shows.

Check your understanding

1   Copy this table. Then complete the second column by putting **one** of the following terms in each box. *(2 marks)*

testosterone	oestrogen	XY	XX

Male chromosomes	
Female hormone	

2   What is meant by the term 'gender identity'? Refer to an example in your answer. *(3 marks)*

3   Distinguish between the terms 'sex identity' and 'gender identity'. *(3 marks)*

AQA Examiner's tip

If you are asked to distinguish between sex identity and gender identity, ensure that you make the difference between the two terms clear. This can be done using the following format:

Sex identity means … whereas gender identity means …

What is the psychodynamic theory of gender development?

The psychodynamic theory was first described by Freud. He believed that we have thoughts and feelings that we are not aware of because they are unconscious.

Objectives

You will be able to:

describe the psychodynamic theory of gender development

describe a study to support the psychodynamic theory of gender development

evaluate the psychodynamic theory of gender development.

Starter activity

1 Freud developed a number of techniques to investigate the unconscious mind. One of these is known as free association.

Work in pairs. One of the pair will read out the following list of words while the other one says the first word that comes into their head when they hear each word.

Freud believed the word that you say shows your unconscious thoughts and feelings. You have five seconds to give your response. If you think about it too much then it is a conscious rather than an unconscious response. Ready? Here are the words:

child	safety	fear	love
father	strong	mother	anger	home

links

See Topic 9.1 for information about the psychodynamic explanation of aggression.

Freud believed that development happens in five stages. The third stage is known as the **phallic stage**, which occurs between the ages of three and five. In this stage, the child unconsciously sexually desires the opposite-sex parent and is jealous of the same-sex parent. In order to deal with these feelings and the anxiety that they produce, the child begins to behave like the same-sex parent. This is known as **identification**. Freud believed this process occurred differently in boys and girls.

■ Gender development in boys

In the phallic stage, a boy is unconsciously attracted to his mother. He is jealous of his father and wants to take his place. He becomes anxious that his father will discover his feelings for his mother and will castrate him. This is known as the **Oedipus complex**. He is therefore torn between the desire he has for his mother and the fear he has of his father. In order to deal with this anxiety and resolve the conflict, he therefore gives up his feelings for his mother and identifies with his father. This means he begins to behave like his father and adopts a masculine gender role by doing the things his father does. He has resolved the Oedipus complex.

Key terms

Phallic stage: Freud's third stage of psychosexual development, in which gender development takes place.

Identification: to adopt the attitudes and behaviour of the same-sex parent.

Oedipus complex: the conflict experienced by a boy in the phallic stage because he unconsciously desires his mother and is afraid of his father.

Freud (1909)

Freud carried out a case study to investigate the gender development of a boy known as 'Little Hans'.

Aim: To investigate Little Hans's phobia.

Method: Hans's father wrote to Freud to tell him about Hans's development. At the age of four Hans developed a phobia of horses. He was frightened that a horse might bite him or fall down. He was particularly afraid of large white horses with black around the mouth. Freud analysed this information.

Results: Freud claimed that Hans was experiencing the Oedipus complex. He unconsciously sexually desired his mother and saw his father as a rival and feared castration. He displaced the fear of his father on to horses. The white horse with black around the mouth represented his father who had a dark beard. His fear of being bitten by a horse represented his fear of castration and his fear of horses falling down was his unconscious desire to see his father dead.

Conclusion: This supports Freud's ideas about the Oedipus complex.

A *Sigmund Freud*

Gender development in girls

In the phallic stage, a girl is unconsciously attracted to her father and is jealous and resentful of her mother. She is worried that her mother will find out about the feelings she has for her father. According to Freud, the girl believes she has already been castrated so she is not as fearful as the boy. She does, however, feel conflict between the feelings she has for her father and the fear of losing her mother's love. This is known as the **Electra complex**. To resolve this, she identifies with her mother and behaves in a similar way to her.

Key terms

Electra complex: the conflict experienced by a girl because she unconsciously desires her father and is afraid of losing her mother's love.

Activity

1. Read back over the psychodynamic theory of gender development and then answer the following questions:

   a. What is the unconscious mind?

   b. In which stage does gender development take place?

   c. What is meant by the 'Oedipus complex'?

   d. How is the Oedipus complex resolved?

   e. Explain how the Little Hans case study supports Freud's ideas about gender development.

AQA Examiner's tip

If the exam question asks you to describe the psychodynamic theory of gender development, you can achieve full marks by accurately describing this process in either boys or girls.

2 Look at the following letter:

> Dear Parenting Magazine
>
> My son Luke is five years old. He used to be very loving towards me but recently he has wanted to spend time with his dad and has started to behave just like him. Why has his behaviour towards me changed?

Answer this letter. Use Freud's ideas to explain why Luke now behaves like his father.

◼ Gender development in a lone-parent household

According to Freud, if a child is brought up in a lone-parent household, he or she will have a poorly developed gender identity. This is because the child does not experience and resolve the Oedipus/Electra complex.

If a boy is raised without a father, he will not develop a masculine gender identity because he has not had a father to identify with during the phallic stage of development. Freud claimed that such a boy would become a homosexual.

Freud claimed that boys raised without a father will have a gender identity problem.

B

Gender disturbance: not developing the gender identity usually associated with one's sex.

Case study

Carl

Rekers (1974) described the case of Carl who was eight years old and had a gender identity problem. He had a feminine voice and liked to talk about topics such as dresses, cosmetics and delivering babies. He preferred to play with girls and frequently played house with his sister. He pretended to be ill or injured rather than play with other boys.

Carl lived with his mother and did not have a stable father figure in his life.

2 Read the case study. Explain possible reasons for Carl behaving in a feminine way. Refer to the psychodynamic theory of gender development in your answer.

Research study

Rekers and Moray (1990)

Aim: To investigate whether there is a relationship between **gender disturbance** and family background.

Method: Researchers rated 46 boys with gender disturbance for gender behaviour and gender identity. Their family background was also investigated.

Results: Of the group, 75 per cent of the most severely gender-disturbed boys had neither their biological father nor a father substitute living with them.

Conclusion: Boys who do not have a father figure present during their childhood are more likely to develop a problem with their gender identity.

C

Activity

3   Work in pairs to answer the following questions:

a   Explain why it is difficult to investigate the unconscious mind.

b   Do you think children can develop a gender identity if they do not have a same-sex parent? Explain your answer.

c   What is the drawback of case studies such as that of Little Hans?

Your answers should help you to understand the following Evaluation.

Evaluation of the psychodynamic theory of gender development

Freud's ideas are very difficult to test because they are based on unconscious thoughts and feelings.

Although there has been a rise in the number of children raised in lone-parent families, there has not been an increase in the homosexual population as Freud suggested would happen. Other psychologists have shown that a wide range of people, not just parents, influence a child's gender development.

There is little evidence to support the idea of the Oedipus and Electra complexes. The Little Hans case study was carried out on one child and therefore the findings cannot be generalised.

Activity

4   Produce a poster showing the key points of the psychodynamic theory of gender development. On your poster include:

a   the key terms

b   the key ideas of Freud's theory

c   a summary of relevant research

d   criticisms of Freud's theory

e   relevant pictures.

Going further

Research who Oedipus was. Explain why Freud used the term 'Oedipus complex'.

Check your understanding

1   Outline what is meant by the 'Oedipus complex'. *(2 marks)*

2   Describe the psychodynamic theory of gender development. Refer to psychological research in your answer. *(5 marks)*

3   Outline at least **one** criticism of the psychodynamic theory of gender development. *(3 marks)*

Objectives

You will be able to:

describe the social learning theory of gender development

describe a study to support the social learning theory of gender development

evaluate the social learning theory of gender development.

Starter activity

1 Look at Photos **A** and **B**. What do they show you about the way that gender development takes place?

A

B

Social learning theory

Social learning theorists believe that gender is learnt from watching and copying the behaviour of others. The processes involved in social learning theory are **modelling**, **imitation** and **vicarious reinforcement**.

Modelling means that an adult, or another child, acts as a role model and provides an example for the child to follow. People who are most likely to be role models for the child include those who are:

- similar to them – friends, same-sex parent
- powerful – teachers, older brothers and sisters
- loving and caring towards the child – parents, teachers.
- Imitation means that the child copies the behaviour shown by the model.
- Vicarious reinforcement means that the child learns from what happens to a role model when that model carries out a particular behaviour. If the model is rewarded for their behaviour, the child is more likely to imitate them, whereas if the model is punished the child is less likely to imitate them.

Key terms

Modelling: a role model provides an example for the child.

Imitation: copying the behaviour of a model.

Vicarious reinforcement: learning from the model's being either rewarded or punished.

Example of social learning

Amir watches his father painting the fence. Amir's father is therefore modelling this behaviour. Amir's mother tells his father that he is doing a good job. Amir gets a paint brush and paints the fence. Amir is therefore imitating his father's behaviour. He has learnt from the praise his father received. This is vicarious reinforcement.

Perry and Bussey (1979)

Aim: To show that children imitate behaviour carried out by same-sex role models.

Method: Children were shown films of role models carrying out activities that were unfamiliar to the children. In one condition, all of the male role models played with one activity while all the female role models played with the other activity. In the second condition some of the male role models and some of the female role models played with one activity while the other male and female role models played with the other activity.

Results: In the first condition, the children imitated what they had seen the same-sex role models doing. The boys chose the activity the male role models had played with while the girls chose the activity the female models had played with. In the second condition, there was no difference in the activities the boys and girls chose.

Conclusion: When children are in an unfamiliar situation they will observe the behaviour of same-sex role models. This gives them information about whether the activity is appropriate for their sex. If it is, the child will imitate that behaviour.

Research study

Activity

2 Read the Perry and Bussey study and answer the following questions:

a Why did the boys and girls in the first condition choose different activities?

b Why was there no difference in the activities chosen by the boys and girls in the second condition?

Now read the following explanation.

Activity

1 Look at the following examples of behaviour:

a Tia observes her sister putting nail varnish on her fingernails. Tia's mother tells her sister that her nails look lovely.

Will Tia imitate her sister's behaviour? Explain your answer. Include the terms 'modelling' and 'vicarious reinforcement'.

b Jack observes his older brother being told off for playing with a doll.

Will Jack imitate his brother's behaviour? Explain your answer.

Explanation

The boys in the first condition imitated the men by choosing the activity the men had chosen. The girls in the first condition imitated the women by choosing the activity the women had chosen. As the men and women had chosen different activites this explains why the boys and girls chose different activities.

In the second condition, the boys and girls again copied the behaviour of the same-sex models. This time, however, as both men and women chose both activities, both boys and girls also chose both activities.

Starter activity

2 Your teacher will record some television adverts for you to analyse. Alternatively you could use advertisements from magazines.

a Draw up a list of gender behaviours.

b Watch the adverts and tally each time you see a man or a woman carry out one of the behaviours you have listed. Your tally chart could look like the example in the margin.

c What do your findings show about gender stereotyping in television adverts?

Behaviours	Males	Females
Doing DIY		
Washing clothes		
Shopping at the supermarket		
Playing football		

■ Media and gender development

The **media** provides models for gender behaviour. Macklin and Kolbe (1984) claimed that children want to imitate characters on television because they are often physically attractive.

Television shows males and females in stereotyped ways. For example, women are shown as housewives, secretaries and nurses while men are shown as doctors, police officers and business managers.

C
D

∞ links

See Topic 4.1 for more about stereotyping.

Did you know ??????

Children in Britain watch an average of 2.6 hours of television each day and 80 per cent of 5–16-year-olds have a television in their bedroom.

Research study

Williams (1986)

Aim: To investigate the effects of television on the gender development of children.

Method: In 1975, Williams studied the effects of television on children living in Canada. At the beginning of the study one of the towns was being provided with television for the first time while the other towns already had television. He measured the attitudes of children living in these towns at the beginning of the study and again two years later.

Results: The children who now had television were more sex stereotyped in their attitudes and behaviour than they had been two years previously.

Conclusion: Gender is learnt by imitating attitudes and behaviour seen on television.

Activity

3 Answer the following questions to help you to understand the evaluation of the social learning theory of gender development:

a This theory is well supported by evidence. Explain why this is a strength of the theory.

b This theory believes that gender differences are all learnt. Explain why this is a weakness of the theory.

Evaluation

- This theory is well supported by research. There are a large number of studies, including those described above, that have found that children learn their gender through the observation and imitation of role models.

- It does not explain why children brought up in one-parent families, without a strong same-sex role model, do not have any difficulty developing their gender.

- It does not explain why two children of the same sex brought up in the same home with the same role models can behave differently. For example, two brothers could be brought up in the same house and have the same group of friends but one could be more masculine in his behaviour than the other.

- This approach believes that gender is learnt, it therefore ignores biological differences between males and females.

Going further

1 Read the following report about the effect of footballers' behaviour on children.

> Boys are influenced by the behaviour of their favourite football players. They will therefore copy the actions they have seen in games on television. If a famous footballer argues with the referee, boys will do the same when they are playing football. If, however, a player is sent off for being aggressive, boys would be less likely to copy because they have seen the negative consequences of this behaviour.

Now answer the following questions.

a Do you agree with what this report is saying? Discuss your ideas with your group.

b Explain how this report supports the social learning explanation of gender.

Activity

4 a Look at the following exam question. Work in pairs to write the answer.

How does social learning theory explain the development of gender in boys and girls? In your answer, include one example of boys' behaviour and one example of girls' behaviour. *(5 marks)*

b Now look at the mark scheme for this question. Did you get full marks?

AO1: This approach argues that children learn to behave as males and females through the processes of observation of models and imitation of these models. If the model is reinforced, imitation is more likely. If the model is punished, imitation is less likely. *(3 marks)*

AO2: Two appropriate examples must be given for two marks. One associated with boys' behaviour and one with girls' behaviour. *(2 marks)*

Check your understanding

1 Outline what is meant by 'vicarious reinforcement'. *(2 marks)*

2 Describe how vicarious reinforcement could affect gender development in a boy. Include **one** example in your answer. *(3 marks)*

3 Describe **one** study carried out to support the social learning theory of gender development. Include in your answer the reason the study was carried out, the method used, the results obtained and the conclusion drawn. *(4 marks)*

4 Outline at least **one** criticism of the social learning theory of gender development. *(3 marks)*

AQA Examiner's tip

When defining a term, do not use the term in your definition. For example, you would not achieve any marks for saying that 'imitation means *imitating someone*'.

8.4 What is the gender schema theory of gender development?

Starter activity

1 Work in pairs. List as many words as you can think of associated with females. These words could include jobs, clothes, hobbies, personality traits and behaviour. Now do the same for males.

a Did you include **gender stereotypes** in your two lists?

b Did you include any of the same words in both lists?

c Do you fit the description you have written for your sex?

Share your ideas with the rest of your group.

Objectives

You will be able to:

describe the gender schema theory of gender development

describe a study to support the gender schema theory of gender development

evaluate the gender schema theory of gender development.

■ What is a gender schema?

A schema is a mental building block of knowledge. It is strengthened or changed as we learn more information from the world around us.

Gender schemas are made up of the knowledge we have about each gender. They contain information about behaviours, clothes, activities, personality traits and roles – those for males and those for females. The gender schemas of some people are made up of gender stereotypes. These could include believing all builders are men and all secretaries are women.

Martin and Halverson (1981) believe that gender schemas develop with age. From the age of two, children know whether they are a boy or a girl. They are able to identify other people as belonging to the same sex as them or belonging to the opposite sex.

Once children are aware that there are two different sexes, they learn about gender from what they see and experience in their environment. At this stage their ideas are rigid and stereotyped. As they get older, however, they gain more knowledge about the world and their gender schemas become more flexible. They learn, for example, that some nurses are men and some footballers are women.

∞ links

See Topic 4.1 for more information on stereotyping.

Key terms

Gender stereotypes: believing that all males are similar and all females are similar.

Gender schema: a mental building block of knowledge that contains information about each gender.

A

B

Martin (1989)

Aim: To show that children's understanding of gender becomes less stereotyped and therefore more flexible as they get older.

Method: Children heard stories about the toys that male and female characters enjoyed playing with. Some of the characters were described as liking gender-stereotyped activities, while other characters were described as liking non-gender-stereotyped activities. The children were then asked to predict what other toys each character would or would not like to play with.

Results: The younger children used only the sex of the character to decide what other toys he or she would or would not like. For example, they would say that a boy character would like to play with trucks even if they had been told that the boy liked playing with dolls. The older children, however, considered both the sex of the character and the other toys that the character enjoyed playing with. For example, they would say that a girl who liked playing with trucks would be less likely to want to play with a doll.

Conclusion: Older children have a more flexible view of gender than younger children do.

Activity

1 In pairs, write two stories that Martin might have used in the study described here. Write one story in which the child plays with gender-stereotyped toys and one in which the child plays with non-gender-stereotyped toys.

By the age of six, children have gained a detailed and complex knowledge of their own gender but know less about the other gender. This is because, once children are able to label themselves as a boy or a girl, they learn which objects, activities and behaviours are associated with each sex. They then concentrate on the things that are appropriate to their own sex and pay less attention to information associated with the opposite sex. For example, a boy might learn that dolls are for girls and so avoid dolls. He will therefore not learn much about them. It is not until children are older that they gain the same level of knowledge about the other gender.

AQA Examiner's tip

When learning definitions, think of an example for each term. This will help you prepare for questions that ask you to outline what is meant by something. Refer to an example in your answer.

C   D

Starter activity

2 Draw a flow diagram to show how gender schemas develop from the age of two.

Individual differences in gender development

Not all children develop gender schemas in the same way. Even as they get older, some children remain highly stereotyped in their ideas. Other children, however, are less stereotyped.

Children who are stereotyped look for information to support their ideas and ignore or remember wrongly information that does not fit their schema. For example, if a child was watching a television programme that showed a conversation between a male and a female nurse, the child would recall both characters as being female. If they then saw a scene between two male doctors they would concentrate on this scene and recall it in detail because it supports their stereotyped idea of **gender roles**. A less stereotyped child would accurately recall the gender roles shown in both scenes.

Research study

Levy and Carter (1989)

Aim: To show that there are individual differences in the way children think about gender.

Method: Children were shown pictures of two toys and asked to choose the one they would like to play with. Sometimes, the toys in the pictures were both stereotypically masculine, sometimes they were both stereotypically feminine and sometimes there was one masculine toy and one feminine toy. These pictures were shown to high and low gender schematised children.

Results: The **highly gender schematised** children chose quickly between the pictures when they were shown one masculine and one feminine toy. If, however, they were shown two masculine toys or two feminine toys they took longer to choose because they either wanted both of the toys or neither of them. The less gender schematised children chose on the basis of personal preference. It therefore took them the same amount of time to choose between the toys on each set of pictures.

Conclusion: Highly gender schematised children choose toys on the basis of whether or not they are appropriate for their sex. Less gender schematised children choose on the basis of their personal preference.

E *A child who is less stereotyped in their ideas about gender*

Key terms

Gender role: behaviour seen as masculine or feminine by a particular culture.

Highly gender schematised: where gender is an important way of thinking about the world so information is organised according to what is gender appropriate and what is gender inappropriate.

Did you know ??????

People who choose non-stereotypical job roles (e.g. women who are engineers) have been found to be less gender stereotyped than people who choose gender stereotyped careers (e.g. women who are nurses).

F

G

2 Gender schemas develop as children learn from their environment. Work in small groups to produce a poster showing examples of information children could learn about gender from their environment.

Evaluation

Many psychologists see this theory as being the most detailed and thorough explanation of gender development. It is well supported by evidence, such as the studies described above. It also has 'intuitive appeal'. This means it fits with our experience.

It does not, however, explain the following:

- why some children are more highly gender schematised than others
- why gender begins to develop at the age of two
- why children choose same-sex friends and gender-appropriate toys before they are able to correctly identify themselves as male or female.

H

3 Each member of your group should write **two** questions about gender. Code the questions as 'easy' or 'difficult'. Stick the questions round the room. Answer as many as you can in a given time limit. Now score the answers. One mark for an easy question answered correctly; two marks for a difficult question answered correctly. There is a prize for the winner.

4 Play 'gender bingo'. Divide a piece of paper into eight squares. In each square, write a term you have learnt in this chapter. Your teacher will read a list of definitions. If your term matches the definition, cross it off. Continue until someone shouts 'bingo'.

1 Do the following to help you to revise this topic:

a Read back over the chapter on sex and gender.

b Do some further research on the key ideas.

c Using the information you have gained, produce:

i revision cards of the key points from this chapter

ii a spider diagram to show how the points link together.

1 Outline what is meant by the term 'gender schema'. *(2 marks)*

2 Identify **one** example of a gender stereotype. *(1 mark)*

3 Describe **one** study to support the gender schema theory of gender development. Include in your answer the reason the study was carried out, the method used, the results gained and the conclusion drawn. *(4 marks)*

4 Outline at least **one** criticism of the gender schema theory of gender development. *(3 marks)*

9.1 What is aggression?

Starter activity

1 In groups, consider the question 'Are we born aggressive, or do we learn to be?' To discuss both sides of the argument, you need to ask yourselves:

a What purpose would it serve if we were born that way (i.e. would it have survival value)?

b If we do learn it, how do we learn?

Discuss your thoughts with other groups.

Biological explanation

If we believe that **aggression** has evolved then we need to establish what mechanisms make us aggressive. One idea is that the cause is our **hormones.** It is widely accepted that males are more aggressive than females. Because of this, hormones are thought to be responsible, as there are large differences between the hormones of men and women. The most obvious hormonal difference is that men have much more testosterone than women. As a result, this hormone is thought to be the cause of aggression in males. This has been supported by the finding that violent criminals have higher levels of testosterone than non-violent criminals.

A second difference between violent and non-violent offenders is a chromosomal abnormality. There is a higher than normal proportion of men with an extra Y **chromosome** amongst violent offenders. When the 23rd chromosome (the sex chromosome) fails to divide, some men end up with an XYY arrangement. This has certain effects, including making men more aggressive than normal.

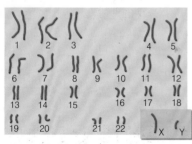

sex chromosomes

A *The 23 pairs of human chromosomes*

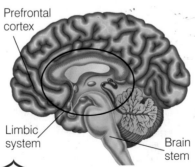

Prefrontal cortex

Limbic system

Brain stem

B *Diagram of the brain, highlighting the limbic system*

Another biological explanation for aggression is that it is caused by an interaction of different parts of the brain. Aggression, like other instinctive behaviour, seems to be associated with the **limbic system**, (see Diagram **B**). This is the part of the brain that influences things

Objectives

You will be able to:

outline the biological explanation of aggression

outline the psychodynamic explanation of aggression

outline the social learning explanation of aggression.

Key terms

Aggression: behaviour aimed at harming others.

Hormones: chemicals released by our endocrine system that affect how our bodies function and how we behave.

Chromosomes: the parts of each cell that carry the genetic information from our parents.

∞ links

See Topic 8.1 for an explanation of sex differences caused by hormones and chromosomes.

AQA Examiner's tip

You will not be required to name the parts of the brain in the exam.

Key terms

Limbic system: the part of the brain that causes aggressive behaviour.

Prefrontal cortex: the very front of the brain. It is involved in social and moral behaviour and controls aggression.

Brain disease: damage to the brain caused by illness or trauma.

like eating, sexual behaviour and aggression. The part of the brain that controls these behaviours and stops us from being aggressive is the **prefrontal cortex**. This is highly involved in learning. It knows when instinctive behaviour is appropriate and when it is not. **Brain disease** affecting either the limbic system or the prefrontal cortex may lead to abnormally high levels of aggression.

Case study

Charles Whitman

In 1966, Charles Whitman climbed up the clock tower at the University of Texas and shot 12 people with a high-powered rifle. This was the last of a series of very aggressive acts he committed throughout his adult life. After he was killed by the Texas Rangers, a post-mortem revealed he had a tumour pressing on the part of his brain that causes aggressive behaviour, the limbic system.

Activity

1   If research has shown that brain damage or other biological factors have led to aggressive behaviour, can we conclude that the person who acts this way is not responsible?

Discuss how you think the law should treat people who are violent if it is not their fault.

■ Psychodynamic explanation

This was proposed by Freud. He suggested we have an unconscious drive that causes aggressive behaviour, just like the unconscious drive that leads to sexual behaviour. Our aggressive behaviour is caused by an internal force, or instinct, which he called **Thanatos**. It is this that drives us towards self-destruction. All the time this instinct is building up inside us, it creates pressure, until sooner or later we cannot control it and it makes us do something aggressive.

Everyone has this instinct towards self-destruction and we protect ourselves by using **ego defence mechanisms**. These redirect our aggression outwardly. So rather than harming ourselves, we will either harm others or redirect our energy into something safe. Two defence mechanisms Freud identified were:

- **displacement** – being aggressive towards other people
- **sublimation** – channelling our aggression into other acceptable activities.

Dollard *et al.* (1939) argued that, although we might have an aggressive instinct building up inside us, Freud was wrong to suggest that it would suddenly spill over into aggressive behaviour for no reason. They said we need something to trigger it off. Think of a loaded gun – it won't fire unless someone pulls the trigger. Dollard *et al.* proposed the frustration–aggression explanation. This claimed that, as well as having an aggressive instinct, we also need something to frustrate us in order to release our aggressive behaviour. Frustration can be caused by ordinary everyday things, such as being late, losing things, or arguments. These things will cause us to release our aggressive instincts and 'let off steam' with aggressive behaviour.

links

See Topic 3.4 for more about the brain and how it can affect personality.

Key terms

Thanatos: the part of our unconscious that causes our aggressive drive.

Ego defence mechanisms: behaviour strategies used by the individual to protect itself.

AQA *Examiner's tip*

Think of Thanatos as a saucepan of boiling water: as the water heats up the pressure forces it over the top. Our aggressive drive does the same: it builds up and up until we can't stop it spilling out.

Activity

2   Sublimation is a way that, Freud believed, we deal with our aggressive instincts by redirecting them into other activities. It is a way of 'letting off steam' in a safer way than by responding to situations in an aggressive manner.

How do you let off steam? In groups draw up a list of ways in which you relieve the tension caused by your aggressive instincts. See if your ways are the same as other people's.

Did you know ??????

Freud only produced his theory of aggression when he was asked to explain the atrocities of the First World War. Before that point he had not given much consideration to aggression.

Who are our role models? Draw up a list of those people whom we are likely to copy in some way. In the first column, write down the people who teach us general behaviour patterns such as attitudes, views about right and wrong, and so on. In the second column, write down the people who teach us specific behaviours, such as the way we dress, catch phrases and even the way we do our hair.

Can you see any differences between the people you have put in the first column and those you have put in the second column?

Social learning theory of aggression

Social learning theory suggests that aggressive behaviour, like all other types of behaviour is caused by people seeing how other people behave, and copying it. As people encounter new situations, they look to other people for guidance as to how they should act. For children, there are lots of new situations, so they are more likely than adults to copy what they see. This is known as 'imitation'.

Social learning theory stresses the importance of **vicarious learning**. We can learn new ways to behave just by watching what other people are doing. This is most clearly demonstrated by young children who swear. The only reason small children will swear is because they have heard someone else do it. It is not something they would do otherwise.

Key terms

Vicarious learning: learning by observation.

Monitoring: judging whether our own behaviour is appropriate or not.

Punishment: a stimulus that weakens behaviour because it is unpleasant and we try to avoid it.

⃝⃝links

See Topic 8.3 on how social learning theory explains gender development.

C *People may copy images of violence that they see on news programmes*

Activity

3 Conduct a survey in which you ask people about what they have watched on television during the previous week. Ask them roughly how long they spend watching television and try to find out how much violence they have seen. You will need to define violence as 'verbal' (e.g. swearing) and 'physical' (e.g. hitting, kicking, or even shooting another person, or damaging property). Put your findings in a table or on a graph to display on the classroom wall.

It has been found that children are more likely to imitate role models if they are similar (e.g. the same age or sex), attractive, powerful or caring. The most important element is if they see the model being reinforced for doing something. If a child sees someone being reinforced for being aggressive, it creates the expectation that they will be reinforced for being aggressive too. It is this expectation that motivates their behaviour. A good example is watching a film in which the hero defeats the villain by hitting him. A child might learn from this that hitting people is a successful way of getting what you want. As a result, aggressive behaviour has been learned.

All the time, people **monitor** their own behaviour. Bandura (1963) realised that not only is reinforcement external but it can also come from inside, in the form of pride or self-satisfaction. We judge our own behaviour. If we feel good about what we have done, this too will strengthen it. In this way, we monitor ourselves. If we feel good about acting aggressively, we will do it again.

One implication of children copying what they see is that **punishment** can actually have the opposite effect to what is intended. Parents are role models, and as such they are more likely than anyone else to be copied by their children. So if a child is hit by his parent, he will learn to hit others just by experiencing this. This means that the parent is (unintentionally) teaching the child aggressive behaviour. Having seen the behaviour of a role model, children will copy it.

∞ links

See Topic 6.2 on operant conditioning for a better understanding of how people react to the consequences of their behaviour (i.e. reinforcement and punishment).

Going further

Research has shown that punishment is not a good way of improving behaviour. In fact, it can lead to an increase in aggression in children. Using a library and/or the internet, see if you can find another reason (apart from the one in the main text) why punishment can lead to aggressive behaviour.

Check your understanding

1 Three approaches that have attempted to explain aggression are:

psychodynamic   biological   social learning

Look at the explanations below and decide which approach is being used. You can choose an approach more than once.

a High levels of the hormone testosterone can cause aggression. *(1 mark)*

b Aggression can be learned by imitating others. *(1 mark)*

c Aggression can be caused by unconscious instincts. *(1 mark)*

d Aggression can be the result of brain damage. *(1 mark)*

e If children observe role models receiving reinforcement for acting aggressively, they are more likely to copy their behaviour. *(1 mark)*

2 Briefly outline how the psychodynamic approach can be used to explain the development of aggression. *(2 marks)*

3 Alfie, who is five years old, is more aggressive than his sister Leone. Their mother tells a friend that, when Leone was five, she was never as aggressive as her brother. How might biological theory explain Alfie's aggression? *(3 marks)*

Objectives

You will be able to:

describe and evaluate studies of the development of aggressive behaviour.

Starter activity

1 See what you can remember about the biological explanations of aggression by trying to match up the following terms with their definitions:

Terms

1 The limbic system
2 Testosterone
3 XYY
4 The pre-frontal cortex

Definitions

a An arrangement of chromosomes that causes aggressive behaviour
b The part of the brain that controls aggressive behaviour
c The part of the brain associated with instincts such as aggression
d The male hormone thought to cause aggressive behaviour

Biological investigations into the causes of aggression

Fifty years ago, research into the development of aggression was conducted on animals. This was because it was impossible to manipulate hormones and explore the brain of humans. Conclusions from the studies were applied to humans.

Research study

Young *et al.* (1959)

Aim: To see what effect hormones have on aggressive behaviour.

Method: Young injected pregnant rhesus monkeys with testosterone and observed the levels of aggression in their offspring as they matured.

Results: The high levels of testosterone during pregnancy made the females grow up to behave like male monkeys – they engaged in rough-and-tumble play and challenged the males for dominance in their troop.

Conclusion: Testosterone does seem to play a vital part in aggressive behaviour.

By the end of the 20th century, as science progressed, techniques had been developed that allowed psychologists to study the human brain directly. One such study was conducted by Raine (1997). He compared the differences between the brains of murderers and non-murderers. He wanted to know if murderers' brains functioned differently, and if this might be the cause of their aggression.

Research study

Raine (1997)

Aim: To investigate the brains of murderers.

Method: Researchers gave 41 murderers in California a **PET scan** and compared them with a similar group of non-murderers.

Results: There were some differences, for example activity in the pre-frontal cortex of the murderers was lower than in non-murderers.

Conclusion: When the pre-frontal cortex (and other parts of the brain) is not working normally, it can lead to people committing violent crimes.

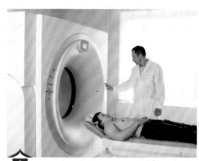

A *A patient being prepared for a brain scan*

So studies of humans and animals have both provided evidence that there are biological causes for aggression: hormones in Young's study and brain disease in Raine's study.

links

See page 14 in Topic 1.2 for a photo of a PET scan of a normal brain.

Activity

1 The studies of Young and Raine illustrate how the biological aspects of aggression are investigated, but there have been many criticisms of these methods.

In groups, identify **three** weaknesses of these studies. You might like to consider who is being studied and how they are being studied. See if you can also think of a positive criticism of these methods: is there an advantage over other methods?

When you have done this, compare your ideas with the other groups' ideas.

AQA Examiner's tip

It must be remembered that whatever conclusions may be drawn from Young's study, we cannot be certain that testosterone has the same impact on humans. This is because he used monkeys. This is a good point of evaluation you could use in the exam.

Other investigations

The frustration–aggression theory was investigated by Barker.

Barker (1941)

Aim: To see the effect of frustration on aggressive behaviour.

Method: Children were kept waiting a long time before being allowed to play in a room full of attractive toys. Their behaviour was then observed.

Results: The children were more aggressive and destructive than other children who had not been frustrated by being kept waiting.

Conclusion: Being frustrated does lead to an increase in aggression.

Research study

Activity

2 In pairs, discuss whether this study could be considered unethical, and if so why.

Freud's theory of aggression has been much harder to support. However, there is some supporting evidence from people who had been unable to stop themselves from becoming aggressive.

Megargee and Mendelsohn (1962)

Aim: To see if there is a link between aggression and personality type.

Method: People who had committed brutally aggressive crimes were interviewed and given personality tests.

Results: These criminals seemed to have been 'over controlled' and **repressed** their anger until it built up to such an extent that it just exploded following something really trivial.

Conclusion: If people do not let their aggressive instinct out in small amounts from time to time, the build-up will be so great that they will not be able to control it.

Research study

Going further

1 If it can be shown that the brains of murderers are abnormal, it could be argued that they are not responsible for killing. In groups, discuss the implications of this. Ask yourselves two questions:

a Are psychologists providing a defence for murderers to use in court?

b If we know someone's brain is abnormal, should we lock them up before they commit murder?

Evaluation

- When the participants of a study are all violent offenders, we have to be careful about applying conclusions to the rest of the population.
- We must remember that people can lie in interviews and personality tests.
- It is difficult to standardise 'frustration'. What is frustrating for one person may not be for another.

2   Refresh your memory of the different parts of social learning theory. Spend five minutes jotting down what is meant by each of the following terms.

a   Vicarious learning   d   Reinforcement
b   Imitation   e   Monitoring
c   Role models

Research based on social learning theory

An important piece of research was undertaken by Bandura (1963) to see if children would copy what they see. He constructed an experiment in a laboratory using an adult role model and a **'bobo' doll**.

Research study

Bandura *et al.* (1963)

Aim: To find out if three- to six-year-old children would imitate the aggressive behaviour they see role models performing towards an inflatable 'bobo' doll.

Method: Researchers divided 96 children into four groups, three of which were shown someone throwing, kicking and punching the 'bobo' doll. Their own behaviour was then observed.

Results: The children who had witnessed the aggressive behaviour showed more aggressive behaviour than the children who had seen none.

Conclusion: Children will copy how they see others behave.

Did you know ??????

In Bandura's experiment, a child was heard to say, 'Look Mummy. There's the doll we're supposed to kick.' This suggests that the child was not acting naturally, as it would outside the laboratory.

Further research in this area was conducted by Liebert and Baron (1972), who wanted to know the effects of watching violence on television.

Research study

Liebert and Baron (1972)

Aim: To see if watching violent television programmes had any effect on aggressive behaviour in children.

Method: One group of children was shown a quite violent television programme, while another was shown an equally exciting sporting event. The two groups were then observed at play.

Results: The group who had watched the violent programme were more aggressive than the group who had watched the sporting programme.

Conclusion: Watching violence on television increases the level of aggression in children's behaviour.

Activity

3   The studies by Bandura and Leibert and Baron were both laboratory-based experiments.

Before reading the Evaluation, divide into groups and think of **three** reasons why the findings from these studies might not be able to explain what happens outside a laboratory. Compare your reasons with those of other groups.

Evaluation

These two studies seem to show that children's aggressive behaviour is affected by what they see. However, it must be remembered that they are both laboratory-based studies and might not reflect what happens in the real world. It may well be that witnessing aggression will not have an effect if the child's parents are present to explain why such behaviour is wrong. After all, when a child is young, its parents are more influential than most other role models.

There is also contradictory evidence concerning the effect of watching aggressive behaviour. The St. Helena Project found that observing more violence does not have any impact on aggressive behaviour in children.

Research study

Charlton *et al.* (2000)

Aim: To see if the introduction of television (and therefore aggressive role models) to a community would affect the aggressive behaviour of children.

Method: For two years after the island of St. Helena first received television transmissions, the behaviour of the children was monitored.

Results: The children did not show any increase in aggressive behaviour.

Conclusion: Merely watching aggressive role models will not be sufficient to make children copy aggressive behaviour.

Evaluation

A positive criticism of this study is that it has high ecological validity. This is because it took place over a two-year period, and the children's behaviour was recorded in their normal surroundings. We can be fairly confident therefore that their behaviour was natural.

Check your understanding

1 Describe **one** study in which aggression was investigated. Include in your answer the reason why the study was conducted, the method used, the results obtained and the conclusion drawn. *(4 marks)*

2 Evaluate the study you have described in your answer to Question 1. *(3 marks)*

3 Read the following statements and decide whether each is **true** or **false**:

   a   The hormone testosterone is thought to increase aggression. *(1 mark)*

   b   Brain damage does not play any part in aggression. *(1 mark)*

   c   Frustration reduces levels of aggression. *(1 mark)*

links

See Topic 5.1 to recap the experimental method and its drawbacks.

Starter activity

1 Match each of the following terms to the correct explanation of aggression.

Explanations

A Biological approach

B Psychodynamic approach

C Social learning approach

Terms

a The limbic system   d Sublimation   g Testosterone

b Thanatos   e Imitation   h Reinforcement

c Vicarious learning   f Frustration   i Extra Y chromosome

Biological methods of reducing aggression

The biological approach believes that since aggressive behaviour is caused by biological factors, the way to reduce it must be to focus on biology too. One such way is with the use of drugs. This is the case with **Attention Deficit Hyperactivity Disorder (ADHD)**. If there is a drug to control ADHD, it should be possible to stop aggressive behaviour. It has been found that the drug **Ritalin**, which stimulates activity in the brain, does reduce the aggressive behaviour caused by ADHD. This is because, when the prefrontal cortex is stimulated, it is able to control the aggressive instincts caused by the limbic system.

Psychosurgery is an alternative method of dealing with brain disease, by either removing or destroying the part of the brain that is not functioning properly. This may be done by inserting a probe to a very precise location and heating up the end to kill the nerves. Because research has shown the limbic system to be responsible for aggressive behaviour, it is usually part of the limbic system that is destroyed. This is used as a last resort because, once brain tissue has been destroyed, it will not grow back. This means that, if a mistake is made with the operation, the consequences are permanent. For this reason, this procedure is not used very often.

A An early technique of performing psychosurgery (1960)

Objectives

You will be able to:

suggest ways of reducing aggression based on the biological, psychodynamic and social learning explanations

evaluate the likely success of each way of reducing aggression.

Activity

1 Organise yourselves into groups and discuss whether you think it is possible to treat a psychological disorder like aggression using the same biological methods that doctors might use to treat physical disorders. Think of the methods that doctors use, and discuss whether you think they would also be successful in the treatment of aggression.

Activity

2 Try to think of at least **two** points of evaluation for each of the two methods outlined above. One point for each method has been given to you already. How many others can you add to the list?

- All drugs have side effects.

- Psychosurgery is irreversible. Once the brain has been destroyed, it won't repair itself.

Key terms

Attention Deficit Hyperactivity Disorder (ADHD): a disorder characterised by short attention span, poor concentration and uncontrollable aggressive outbursts.

Ritalin: a drug used to control Attention Deficit Hyperactivity Disorder (ADHD).

Psychosurgery: an operation on the brain to remove or destroy the part that is causing abnormal behaviour.

Catharsis: the process of getting rid of your emotions by watching other people experiencing emotion.

■ Psychodynamic methods of reducing aggression

Freud suggested two ways of dealing with our aggressive instincts. One is to redirect them into other, safe activities using ego defence mechanisms such as displacement and sublimation. The other is to release them through **catharsis**. Playwrights in ancient Greece filled their plays with murders and other unpleasant things. This was because they believed that, if people watched this on stage, it would 'get it out of their system'. As a result they might be less likely to commit murder themselves. Freud agreed with this principle because it fitted in with his idea about aggression being caused by a build-up of instincts. So, in the modern world, Freud would suggest, it is a good thing to watch violence on television and in films, because it is cathartic; it gets aggressive instincts out of your system.

Another way Freud thought we could release aggressive instincts is by finding a safe activity for ourselves that requires a certain amount of energy. This is called 'sublimation'. If we can put energy into a safe activity, such as sport, it will reduce the build-up of our aggressive instincts. This will make it less likely that we will suddenly have an aggressive outburst for no apparent reason.

B   *Martial arts are useful for the sublimation of aggressive instincts*

> ### *Did you know* ??????
>
> - Thanatos, which is the word Freud used for the aggressive instinct, is a Greek word meaning 'death'.
> - Catharsis was a Greek idea, which meant to purify yourself by experiencing great emotion.

Activity

3   In groups, think of the activities you do for pleasure. Do you think they help you to release your aggressive urges?

Make a list of all the things the members of your group do. Then put them in order of which you think will help you to cope with your aggressive instincts the best. If your list is similar to other groups' lists, put a list of the top five activities on the wall, together with an explanation of how they reduce aggression in people.

Activity

4   Freud's theories are based very much on concepts that are difficult to support with evidence. Can you think why this might not be a good thing for psychologists who are trying to find ways of reducing aggression?

Evaluation

The frustration–aggression theory suggests the best way to reduce aggression is to avoid situations that cause frustration. This can be difficult because very often you are not in control of those things that cause frustration, such as your favourite football team losing. However, the theory argues that, since it is frustration that causes an outburst of aggressive behaviour, avoiding frustration is still the most effective way of avoiding aggression.

These explanations sometimes conflict (as you will see in the next section). For example, if you are at a football match and your team loses, you will become frustrated and therefore aggressive. However, according to the biological explanation, if your team wins, there will be an increase in your testosterone level and you will also become aggressive.

Activity

5   In groups, make a list of situations that cause you to become frustrated. For each situation discuss how this could be avoided. Do you think it is possible to avoid most frustration?

2 See if you can remember the different parts of social learning theory. Provided below are some definitions. For each one, provide the name of the thing being described:

a the inflatable doll Bandura used to study how children copy behaviour

b the way children learn by observation

c strengthens behaviour when it happens after you have done something

d someone children copy (e.g. parents, friends or actors)

e when people judge their own behaviour as either good or bad.

■ Social learning method of reducing aggression

Since social learning theory stresses the influence of role models in what we learn, it seems obvious that the way to reduce aggression will be to observe more non-aggressive role models. Or it might be sufficient to see a role model being punished for being aggressive. This second idea was tested by Bandura.

Key terms

Curvilinear: a relationship that increases in strength to a point, but then begins to decrease.

Did you know ??????

The more violence a child watches on television when it is young, the more aggressive it will be when it becomes a teenager. However, the relationship is **curvilinear** – children who watch an excessive amount of violence do not become the most aggressive teenagers.

Research study

Bandura (1965)

Aim: To see if observing a role model being punished would reduce the chance of aggression being copied.

Method: Children were shown an adult model either being punished or reinforced for acting aggressively.

Results: Those children who saw the model being punished were less aggressive themselves than those who saw the model reinforced.

Conclusion: If children see that aggression brings a punishment, they will not copy it.

C *Punishment*

Evaluation of Bandura's study

At first glance Bandura's conclusion seems to be reasonable. However, it was also found that when the children themselves received reinforcement for being aggressive, they *all* copied the aggression that they had seen earlier. This suggests that children know some behaviour is wrong, but will copy it anyway when they think there will be no punishment for them.

AQA Examiner's tip

It is worth remembering that in the exam you can use ethics as a way of evaluating the success of these methods of reducing aggression.

Activity

6 Think once again who our role models are. Imagine a concerned parent asking you for advice about reducing the aggressive behaviour of her young child.

What would you suggest she do, based on social learning theory? Think about the ideal behaviour of other family members around the child and which other role models the child might be exposed to.

Make a list of suggestions, and compare your list with those of others in your group.

People monitor their behaviour and judge whether what they (and others) are doing is good or bad. Because of this, social learning theory would suggest that it is possible to reduce aggression by getting people to think differently about how to behave. Huesmann *et al.* tested this theory.

Huesmann *et al.* (1983)

Aim: To see if teaching children to think more carefully about what they see would reduce aggression.

Method: A group of children was taught to realise that what happens on television is not real. The camera sometimes depicts things that do not happen, and people mostly use non-violent methods of resolving problems. The children's behaviour was then compared with that of another group of children who did not receive any training.

Results: The children who received training showed less aggression than the other group.

Conclusion: Aggression can be reduced by making children think about how they behave so that role models on television become less influential.

Research study

Evaluation of Huesmann's study

The problem with applying this training outside the experiment is that many parents would have difficulty explaining such psychological ideas to their children. Firstly, parents do not have the training to explain concepts in a way children can understand. Secondly, parents are not always present when children are watching television to be able to discuss the programmes afterwards.

Activity

7   Social learning theory advises that, to reduce aggression, children should not be exposed to aggressive role models on television. Freud would advise that, through 'catharsis', watching aggressive role models will reduce aggression.

Which of these two views seems right to you? Divide yourselves into two groups and have a debate about this issue. Your teacher should judge which group makes the better arguments.

Check your understanding

1 Use your knowledge of the psychodynamic approach to discuss one way of reducing aggression. *(4 marks)*

2 Discuss the likely success of the biological approach to reducing aggression. *(4 marks)*

3 Outline **one** method of reducing aggression using social learning theory. *(2 marks)*

Going further

Many psychologists have written about the effects of television on aggressive behaviour. What effect do you think television (any television, not just violence) has on aggressive behaviour according to the theories you have just been reading about? For each term, decide between 'good effect', 'bad effect' or 'no effect':

■ chromosomal abnormality

■ hormones

■ brain disease

■ psychodynamic theory

■ frustration–aggression theory

■ social learning theory.

In each case, can you explain why?

10 Further research methods

10.1 What survey methods can be used?

This chapter builds on your knowledge and understanding of the content of Chapter 5, Research Methods. Although you will not be asked questions about the experimental method in the Unit 2 examination, you will need to revise your understanding of the following:

- target populations, samples and sampling methods: random; opportunity; systematic and stratified; see Topic 5.2 on page 76
- calculations including mean, mode and median, range and percentages; anomalous results and their possible effects; see Topic 5.3 on page 78
- graphical representations, including bar charts; see Topic 5.3 on page 81
- ethical issues in psychological research as outlined in the British Psychological Society guidelines; see Topic 5.4 on page 82
- ways of dealing with each of these issues; see Topic 5.4 on page 82.

Objectives

You will be able to:

understand the survey methods of questionnaires and interviews

understand closed and open questions and structured and unstructured interviews

understand the advantages and disadvantages of questionnaires and interviews, including ecological validity.

Starter activity

1 This activity will help you to think about the research methods you studied in Unit 1.

Copy out the following passage and fill in the gaps using some of these terms:

ethical issues   random allocation   hypothesis

sample   independent variable   median

experiments   participants   cause

Psychologists often carry out _____ in order to find out about the relationship between a _____ and an effect. In the investigation, an _____ will be altered by the researcher in order to see if there is a change in the dependent variable. The researcher will identify a target population and then select a _____ of people to take part in the investigation. The results from the sample will help the researcher to support or reject the _____. Researchers must take _____ into account when carrying out an investigation to make sure that participants are treated with respect.

Key terms

Questionnaire: a set of standard questions about a topic that is given to all the participants in the survey.

Survey: a method used for collecting information from a large number of people by asking them questions, either by using a questionnaire or in an interview.

Closed question: a question where the possible responses are fixed, often as 'yes' or 'no' options.

1 Many people believe that videogames and many television programmes are violent and that they have increased aggressive behaviour in young people. Your task is to design a **questionnaire** about this issue. You should work in small groups of three or four people. The questionnaire needs to have 10 questions in total. Your group should try to answer each question, to make sure that it will collect the information you need.

When you have finished, you should present your questionnaire to the other groups to see if there are many different questions or whether the questions are similar to each other. Make sure each member of your group has a copy of the final questionnaire.

1 ☐
2 ☐
3 ☐
4 ☐
5 ☐
6 ☐
7 ☐
8 ☐
9 ☐
10 ☐

Questionnaires

A questionnaire is an example of a **survey** method that is used to collect large amounts of information from a group of people who are often spread out across the country. The researcher must design a set of questions that the people who take part in the survey (the **respondents**) will answer. All the respondents will answer all the questions and the researcher must try to make sure that the answers given provide information that is needed for the investigation.

There are different types of questions that can be used on a questionnaire. Each type produces a different type of information.

Closed questions

Closed questions are questions where the range of possible answers is determined by the researcher. The respondents are required to tick a box or underline/circle the answer that fits their response. Examples of three closed questions are shown in the margin box.

Examples of closed questions

For each of these questions, underline the answer that most closely applies to you.

1	Are you female?	Yes/No
2	Do you watch TV?	Never/Sometimes/Often
3	Do you play videogames?	Never/Sometimes/Often

Closed questions provide the researcher with data that are easy to collate or put together. The researcher can work out quite quickly the percentages of people who responded 'Yes/No' or 'Never/Sometimes/Often'. Then a bar chart can display the responses graphically.

However, there is little detail in the answers given. Also, because the respondents do not have the opportunity to explain their answers, the researcher does not know why they chose that particular response. Another problem can be that the respondents are not sure exactly what the difference between 'Sometimes' and 'Often' might be, so they choose 'Sometimes' as a *safe* answer. The same thing often happens when people are given 'Don't know' as an option. They pick it because they do not want to give a definite answer of either 'Yes' or 'No'.

A *Answering a questionnaire containing closed questions*

Starter activity

2 You need to get a written answer to the following question: 'How do you feel when you play a videogame? Explain your answer.'

You can answer the question yourself if you play videogames or ask a friend or someone else in your group who likes playing videogames.

What do you notice about the responses to the question when you check with the rest of the class?

Open questions

Open questions are questions where the respondent can write an individual answer and they are given space to do this. The answers to these questions provide lots of detail. The respondents are able to explain their answers so they feel less frustrated than when they have to choose an answer that might not fit exactly what they want to say. These questions provide the researcher with lots of information about behaviour, often with explanations for why a person has produced a particular behaviour. However, problems can occur when open questions are used on a questionnaire. It is very hard to collate, or group together, all the individual responses into an overall pattern because each response is different. Sometimes researchers have to produce categories of responses and fit the individual answers into these categories. However, this will mean the detail and depth of information in the individual responses is lost because the researcher has tried to summarise the findings.

Examples of open questions

Answer each of these questions as clearly as you can.

1 What kinds of TV programmes do you watch and why do you choose these?
2 Why do you enjoy playing videogames?
3 How would you answer someone who says videogames are too violent?

Further issues to consider when writing questions

Another issue is that it is very important for the researcher to be sure the questions are clear and **unambiguous**. The words used in the question should not be emotive because this might upset the person filling in the questionnaire and affect the honesty of their answers. Also, the meaning of the question must be obvious to the reader. When questions are unambiguous their meaning is absolutely clear. This means that the respondents are sure of exactly what the question is asking and exactly how to give an answer to the question. This will increase the **ecological validity** of the questionnaire. The researcher can be confident that the answers are a true account of the behaviour of the respondents.

Key terms

Open question: a question where the person answering can give any response they like.

Unambiguous: something that has only one meaning.

Ecological validity: the results of the investigation can be said to apply to real-life behaviour. They are an accurate account of behaviour in the real world.

Activities

2   Look at the following questions. Can you see what the problems might be with the way they have been written?

a   How many hours a week do you spend playing videogames?
   Up to 1 hour   2–3 hours   More than 5 hours

b   Playing videogames is a waste of time and makes people aggressive.
   Agree   Disagree

3   Now look at the questionnaire you designed on the issue of videogames and television and their possible effects on aggression.

Check through the questions you wrote. Did your group make either of the mistakes that can be seen in the previous activity? You need to make sure that the questions you have asked can all be answered easily. They should provide your respondents with the opportunity to tell you accurately what they know, think and feel about the issue.

Did you know ??????

Many questionnaires are sent out by post and the return rate can vary between 5 per cent and 54 per cent. This means that the results of a questionnaire might reflect the answers of a very small group of people who do not represent the population. The results cannot be generalised.

Advantages and disadvantages of questionnaires

The main advantage of using questionnaires to find out about behaviour and attitudes is that a great deal of data can be collected quickly. That is why large organisations often use questionnaires to get feedback quickly from their customers. Closed and open questions both have advantages and disadvantages, so it is often useful to have both types in a questionnaire. Closed questions are easy to score and open questions provide detailed information. Open questions allow people to explain their answers so the researcher knows why the particular answer has been given. Questionnaires are ethical because people are fully aware that they are filling in the questionnaire and they know what the questions are asking.

There are some disadvantages, however. Questionnaires provide the answers respondents want to give and there is no way of checking that the answers are actually true. This means the results of the questionnaire could be misleading for the researcher.

B

3 A researcher wanted to find out students' feelings about the use of mobile phones both in and outside school. She decided to write a questionnaire to collect the information she required.

a Write **one** open question that might be used to find out about a student's use of a mobile phone in school.

b Write **one** closed question that might be used to find out about a student's use of a mobile phone in school.

Interviews

Interviews involve the researcher in direct contact with the respondent, who in this case is called the **interviewee**. This is often face-to-face contact but could be over the telephone. The vast majority of interviews involve a questionnaire and the researcher can record the answers at the time of the interview. Alternatively, they can record the interview itself and then play back the content later to analyse the responses. Interviews are not a just a 'chat', even though they usually involve two people talking to each other. They are focused on a particular topic.

C Interviews often involve face-to-face contact

4 Many students believe that mobile phones are an essential item both in and out of school or college. Your task is to design a set of eight questions about this. You should work in small groups of three or four people. Your group should make sure that the questions you ask will get you the information you need.

When you have finished you should present your interview questions to the other groups to see if there are many different questions or whether the questions are similar to each other. Make sure each member of your group has a copy of the final interview questions.

There are two types of interview:

- **Structured interview** – in this type of interview the questions are all pre-set and every interviewee will be asked exactly the same questions in the same order. The researcher cannot ask an extra question based on an interesting point made by the interviewee. It is usually the case that the questions are *closed* but some may be *open*.

- **Unstructured interview** – in this type of interview the researcher will have decided on the topic and may have a starter question, but the next question will be based on the response made by the interviewee. This means that each person interviewed will have a different set of questions and it is the interviewee who directs the discussion.

Activity

5 It is important to think about the advantages and disadvantages of the different types of interview methods. In groups of three or four, write down **one** advantage and **one** disadvantage of:

a   structured interviews

b   unstructured interviews.

Look back over your notes on questionnaires to help you.

Advantages and disadvantages of interviews

In general, interviews produce large amounts of data. They provide information about people's thoughts and feelings that cannot be found out by just watching behaviour. The data from structured interviews can be collated and analysed easily. The data from unstructured interviews are detailed and have ecological validity.

The disadvantages of the interview method are similar to those of the questionnaire method. The researcher cannot be sure the interviewee is telling the truth, so the data may not be accurate.

Structured interviews lack detail and may be frustrating for:

- the interviewer, who wants to ask another question
- the interviewee, who cannot explain the answer they have given.

Data from unstructured interviews may be difficult to collate and analyse.

Check your understanding

1   What is a survey? *(2 marks)*

2   Distinguish between each of the following:

a   closed questions and open questions *(3 marks)*

b   structured interviews and unstructured interviews. *(3 marks)*

3   State **one** advantage and **one** disadvantage of conducting surveys in psychology. *(2 marks)*

Going further

You might like to try to interview someone about the use of mobile phones by students in your school or college. If you work in small groups you need to decide whether your group will use either a structured or an unstructured interview. Make sure each person in the group has a copy of the questions. Those who decide to use an unstructured interview will need to keep a record of the questions that were asked. Each person in the group should interview one person and bring the results back to the group. Each group should analyse the results and present the findings to the class. What did you discover:

- about mobile phone use
- about interviewing people.

Remember to be sensitive when you ask your questions.

AQA Examiner's tip

When you are answering questions about the advantages or disadvantages of questionnaires and interviews, you must make it clear whether you are referring to open or closed questions in a questionnaire, or to structured or unstructured interviews.

10.2 What are observation studies?

Starter activity

1 Imagine you want to know how people behave at pedestrian crossings. In particular, you would like to find out if they obey the 'red man' or not and if there are any gender differences in pedestrian-crossing behaviour. You could carry out a survey and ask people what they do at pedestrian crossings.

a What might be the problem if you did this?

b Can you think of another way that you might be able to collect data about pedestrian-crossing behaviour?

Observational method

In this method the researcher decides to watch behaviour as people produce it. Researchers want to be certain that the behaviour they are recording is 'normal' behaviour and seeing the behaviour occur naturally is one way of making sure that this is the case. In most **natural observations**, people are observed in their usual environments and the researcher does not interfere with the location at all. Sometimes, researchers do make something happen so that the natural responses of people can be recorded. One example of this can be seen in a study by Hofling *et al.* (1966).

While on duty, a nurse received a telephone call from a 'doctor' in psychiatry who instructed the nurse to give medicine to a patient on the ward. The researchers watched the nurse to see if she obeyed the illegal instruction or refused. (Nurses are not allowed to give medicine if the instruction comes from a phone call.) As far as the nurses in the study were concerned, the setting was their normal place of work, so their behaviour was natural, but the researchers had changed a very small part of the environment (they introduced the phone call) so they could be there to watch what happened.

Imagine if you had decided to conduct an observation of bystander behaviour. If you wanted to find out whether people help when someone drops their shopping, there are several possibilities:

- You could stand in the street hoping someone might drop their shopping, which is not very likely to happen.
- You could bump into someone and hope their shopping drops, which is not acceptable.
- You could ask a confederate or co-researcher to drop some shopping near to where you are in the street and you could record the actions of the pedestrians.

Objectives

You will be able to:

understand observation studies including categories of behaviour

understand inter-observer reliability and how to establish it

understand the advantages and disadvantages of observation studies.

Key terms

Natural observation: watching the behaviour of people who are in their usual environment.

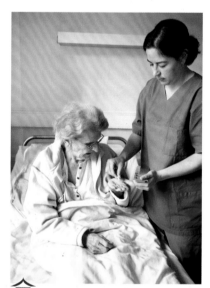

A *A nurse giving medicine*

⚭links

See page 106 in Topic 7.2 for more about Hofling's study of obedience.

See also Topic 7.5 and Topic 7.6 for studies of bystander behaviour.

Sometimes an **observation study** is conducted in a laboratory setting. This is not necessarily a laboratory. It just means that the place where the observation is carried out has been organised by the researcher to make it easy for the observation to be conducted. Therefore, the people being observed are brought into a special room where they can be seen and recorded. This kind of observation might lack ecological validity as the people being observed know that the study is taking place.

Categories of behaviour

In order to make sure that an accurate record of behaviour can be made, researchers use a **categories of behaviour** system. In an observation of playground behaviour, the target behaviour is 'playground behaviour'. However, the observers would not know what they were to look for if that was the only information they had. Behaviour categories are used to make it clear exactly how to record the actions that have been seen. For the playground study, suitable categories would be as shown in Table **D**.

Key terms

Observation study: a method of collecting information about behaviour by watching and recording people's actions.

Categories of behaviour: the separate actions that are recorded as examples of the target behaviour.

AQA Examiner's tip

Remember, if a question asks you to explain a term, you cannot use that term in your answer. Candidates often write, 'Observation *studies* are studies in which the behaviour of people is *observed*.' This will not gain credit. You need to write about 'investigations in which the behaviour of people is watched and recorded'.

B Hopscotch

C Skipping

D A tally chart showing categories of behaviour for observation of playground behaviours in boys and girls

	Categories of behaviours			
	Running	Hopping	Skipping	Standing
Boys	⊪⊪⊪	‖			‖
Girls	‖‖	⊪‖‖	⊪‖‖		

Activity

1 In pairs, design a record sheet containing behavioural categories you could use to record the behaviour of males and females at a pedestrian crossing. You need to think of all the ways people could use the crossing and then create categories for the behaviours you want to record. Remember, pedestrian crossings have red and green lights that are supposed to control the way people use them.

Compare your record sheet with those of other pairs.

E A pedestrian crossing

Starter activity

2 In groups, list **three** advantages and **three** disadvantages of the observational method.

Advantages and disadvantages of the observational method

The observational method is usually very high in ecological validity. For many of the behaviours that humans produce, especially social behaviours, this method is the most sensible way of finding out about what people really do. Milgram (1963) found that, if you ask people what they would do, they often provide misleading information. All the people he interviewed said they would not complete his study, but in the experiment over 60 per cent of his participants did complete it.

F *Observation can be carried out by watching people from a distance*

G *Is one of the group observing the non-verbal communication of the others?*

Observation studies record real behaviours that are full actions. Many people criticise memory research because the participants learn lists of words and this is a very small behaviour that hardly relates to the person at all. Observation studies record whole behaviours that people really do produce regularly.

There are still some disadvantages because, although researchers can see and record the behaviour, they do not know *why* it occurred. An observer might make a mistake when recording the behaviour so the record sheet might be inaccurate. Also, the people who are being watched might become aware of this and change their behaviour. This would affect the accuracy of the results. There are often ethical issues involved when people are not aware that they are being watched. Finally, observation studies can be difficult and time-consuming to carry out.

Activity

2 a There is a possible problem with the data that the researcher will have collected by the end of the observation period. It may not be accurate. Can you think of any reasons why this might be the case? Discuss this with the rest of your group.

b Researchers have to find a solution to this problem. Can you think of anything they could do to make sure their record of the observation period is accurate?

⚭ links

See Topic 5.1 for information about ecological validity.

See Topic 7.2 for more about Milgram's study of obedience.

Did you know ??????

The information about carrying out observation studies in this chapter has concentrated on the researcher observing people from a separate location. This is called 'non-participant observation'; the researcher does not participate in the behaviour but watches from a distance.

⚭ links

See Topic 5.4 for a discussion of ethical issues.

Did you know ??????

There is a method of observation called 'participant observation' in which the researcher becomes a member of the group or institution they are observing. One researcher became a teacher in a school for many months so that he could observe the relationships between pupils and teachers. Can you think of any ethical issues that might be involved in such a study?

Inter-observer reliability

When an observation study has been conducted, the record of the behaviours that have been watched has to be an accurate record. The researcher needs to be sure that, every time a behaviour that fits the behavioural categories occurs, it is recorded. This can be a major problem because in many observation studies the actual behaviour will have passed, so it cannot be seen again.

A solution to this problem is to use the following procedure:

- The researcher designs a record sheet with suitable behaviour categories for the observation they wish to conduct.
- Two observers each have a copy of the *same record sheet* and watch the *same behaviour/location* at the *same time* for the *same period of time*, recording what they see on their own individual record sheet.
- At the end of the observation period the observers compare their record sheets.

If they have been recording consistently, they will have matching or very similar records of the observation they have carried out. This means they will have established **inter-observer reliability**. If the two record sheets are very different, then both will have to be discarded. This is because it would not be possible to work out which observer's record was the accurate one.

Activity

3 This is your chance to see if you can observe and record behaviours accurately. Go back to the record sheet you and your partner designed for the pedestrian-crossing behaviour of males and females. You can either choose to carry out this observation study or design a study that is more appropriate for your local environment. This might mean watching people in a shopping centre where you could look at whether men and women carry their shopping bags differently, or how they hold the door open for people following them into and out of shops. You might look at non-verbal behaviour in cafes.

Use what you now know about carrying out an observation study and how to establish inter-observer reliability. Make any changes you feel are necessary to your record sheets or design new ones that are more appropriate to your new observation study.

Check your understanding

1 Explain **one** reason why observation studies can be said to have ecological validity. *(3 marks)*

2 Two psychologists conducted an observation study of males and females parking their cars in a supermarket car park. Explain why the psychologists decided that they should both record the behaviour of the drivers. *(3 marks)*

3 Briefly discuss **one** ethical issue that might occur in an observation study. *(3 marks)*

Key terms

Inter-observer reliability: when this is high, the records made by more than one observer in a study are considered to be accurate because they match or are very similar to each other.

AQA Examiner's tip

Sometimes candidates think that having two observers means that, if one observer misses a behaviour, the other will spot it and that would be a 'good thing.' In fact, that would not make the observation reliable. In order to achieve high inter-observer reliability, both observers should consistently record the behaviours every time they occur.

Going further

1 a Conduct your observation study using the materials that you have designed. Then prepare a short report of what you did, what your findings were and what patterns of behaviour, if any, you discovered.

b When you have heard the reports of other pairs who carried out an observation similar to yours, discuss the results together. Consider the data collected overall. Were there any similar patterns of behaviour found by the groups? If there were differences, can you think of why these might have occurred?

c Did any of the pairs of record sheets match? Was there any inter-observer reliability in the record sheets in your class?

What are case studies?

Starter activity

So far, all the methods of investigation we have looked at have involved studying the behaviour of groups of people. This is because researchers often want to find explanations of human behaviour that can be applied to all people. However, there are times when researchers want to focus their attention on unique individuals, whose behaviour is not usual.

In small groups of three or four, discuss what kinds of behaviours produced by *individual* people would be of interest to psychologists.

Case study method

A **case study** is an in-depth investigation of an individual or of a unique group. Case studies are carried out by professional psychologists who work in environments such as hospitals, prisons or therapy centres. The information can be from a number of sources. These include *interview* details about the person's life – these are *biographical* details. There might also be work records or school records if the person is a child. The psychologist might carry out *observations* of the person or *test* the person using some kind of scale, such as a personality test.

Sometimes a case study will be carried out to add to our understanding of human behaviour in general rather than our understanding of a particular person. The case study is written up as a description of the individual. The psychologist will then interpret the information using psychological theory to decide how to use the information collected. If the case study is of a single person this will usually involve what treatment should be offered. Otherwise it will be used to support or challenge a theory.

A famous case study was conducted by Richard Gregory and Jean Wallace (1963). They investigated a man who had been blind from infancy, but whose sight was restored by an operation when he was an adult. Gregory and Wallace discovered that the man was not affected by visual illusions. Gregory used this information to support his theory that visual perception in humans is affected by experience of the world.

A *Conducting a case study*

Objectives

You will be able to:

understand the method of case studies

understand the advantages and disadvantages of case studies.

Key terms

Case study: an in-depth investigation of an individual, a small group or an organisation.

Activity

1 Choose a famous psychologist whose work you have enjoyed studying while you have been taking your GCSE course. Think about the theories and/or the research this person produced and why you were interested in the information. Imagine you have the opportunity to meet with that psychologist. What questions would you ask him or her? What kinds of information would you want to get from this meeting? Write down some examples of:

a the personal information you might ask about

b the questions about the work of the psychologist that you might ask

c any other information you would require, such as how their work affected their life.

Do you think you would enjoy the opportunity to do this kind of research? Discuss this with your group.

Gregory found that the man whose sight was restored did not think the vertical lines in the Ponzo illusion (Diagram **B**) were of different lengths. Whereas most people who look at the diagram do believe the vertical line on the right is longer than the vertical line on the left.

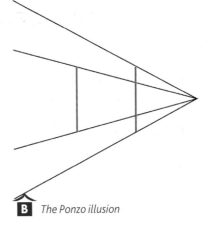

B *The Ponzo illusion*

Activity

2 Think about the procedures involved in conducting a case study. Discuss with a partner the possible advantages of using this method to find out about behaviour. What are the disadvantages of using this method?

You should be able to write down **two** advantages and **two** disadvantages of the case study method. Don't read ahead until you have attempted this activity.

Advantages and disadvantages of case studies

The following list highlights some of the main advantages of the case study method:

■ Case studies provide detailed information about individuals rather than collecting just a score on a test from a person.

■ Case studies record behaviour over time so changes in behaviour can be seen.

■ A single case study that shows us that a theory is not correct is very useful. It will encourage researchers to change the theory and make it more accurate.

There are some disadvantages too:

■ The data collected can be very subjective. The method relies on the individual who is being studied remembering events and these memories might not be accurate or reliable. Also, the interpretations made by the psychologist could be biased and therefore the content of the case study might be unreliable.

■ The information from the case study cannot be applied to anyone else because it is unique.

■ There are ethical issues, especially of confidentiality, right to withdraw and protection from harm. The last might occur because very often the person being studied is someone who is suffering from psychological problems. This means they could be vulnerable.

AQA *Examiner's tip*

Remember, case studies are carried out by professional psychologists so you should not attempt to conduct a case study of your own. However, in the examination you might be asked how or why a psychologist might carry out a case study.

Going further

This is your chance to do some research. There are some famous studies of individuals in psychology. Sigmund Freud wrote accounts of individuals including Little Hans, the Rat Man, Dora and the Wolf Man. Other famous investigations have been carried out, studying 'Genie' and 'HM'.

Use the internet and other library resources to research at least one of these individuals and any others you might discover. You can then present your findings about these people to the rest of your group.

Check your understanding

1 Give **two** reasons why a psychologist might choose to investigate behaviour using the case study method. *(2 marks)*

2 Identify **one** ethical issue that might arise in the case study method. *(1 mark)*

3 Explain how an issue you identified in Question 2 could be dealt with by the researcher. *(2 marks)*

10.4 What is a correlation?

Starter activity

1   Every member of your group should write their height and their foot size in centimetres on a piece of paper. (You can measure everyone against a wall in the room to get their heights and each person can draw round their foot on a piece of paper and measure the length that way.)

Write the pairs of measurements for each person on the board. Do you notice any pattern in the data you have collected? Can you think of any way of displaying the data using a graph?

Correlation in psychology

Sometimes, researchers are interested in seeing if there is a particular kind of **relationship** between two **variables**. In an experiment the relationship is a 'cause and effect' one. Changing one variable, such as the amount of noise, has an effect on the other variable, such as the number of words someone recalls.

There are times when the researcher does not change or manipulate a variable. Instead two variables are just measured and the researcher looks at how they are related to each other. These variables could be behaviours that people produce, such as the number of cigarettes people smoked in a year and the number of colds those people had in the same year. They could also be qualities, such as how happy a person would rate themselves to be and how motivated they are at work. Psychologists use **correlation** to try to establish whether or not there is a pattern in the connection between the two variables.

Correlation is not a research method; it is a statistical technique that is used to analyse the possible association between two variables. Each variable has to be measured as a score or value of some sort. These scores can then be plotted on a special graph called a **scatter graph**. To produce a scatter graph the data have to be collected in pairs. Usually each person in the study provides a pair of scores, one score for each variable being measured. In the Starter activity, each member of your group provided two measurements: their height and foot size.

How to plot a scatter graph

To draw a scatter graph, the horizontal axis (x-axis) represents the scale for one variable, such as foot size in centimetres, and the vertical axis (y-axis) represents the scale for the other variable, such as height in centimetres. For each pair of scores, you find the point on the x-axis that represents the foot size and find the point on the y-axis that represents the height. Where the lines intersect, put a dot or cross on the graph. This means that each point or cross on the graph represents a pair of measurements.

Objectives

You will be able to:

understand what is meant by 'correlation'

understand the advantages and limitations of correlations.

Key terms

Relationship: a connection between two or more variables.

Variable: a factor or thing that can change – it varies.

Correlation: a technique used by researchers to establish the strength of a relationship between two variables.

Scatter graph: a graph for representing correlations.

AQA Examiner's tip

Don't forget that some of the information you learned in Unit 1 will be required to answer questions in Unit 2. This information has been identified at the start of this chapter.

If you look back to Chapter 5, you will find the information on samples and sampling, calculations, graphical displays and ethics. Make sure that you revise these topics again for the Unit 2 examination.

Your teacher will practise methods questions with you and you will see how the information in these further research methods is used.

Activity

1 Plot a scatter graph to display the data collected in the Starter activity. Remember to give your graph a title that refers to the relationship between both of the variables.

Key terms

Positive correlation: a relationship between two variables in which, as the value of one variable increases, the value of the other variable also increases.

Positive correlation

Graph **A** shows a **positive correlation**. In a positive correlation, as the value of one variable increases so does the value of the other variable. The scatter graph shows that, as the number of umbrellas being carried by people increases, the number of puddles on the ground increases. These two patterns are found to occur at the same time. Remember, the positive correlation does not tell us what causes this relationship, only that the relationship can be identified.

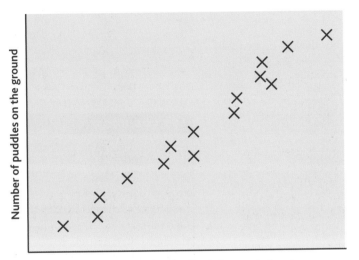

Number of umbrellas being carried

 A *Scatter graph showing positive correlation*

B

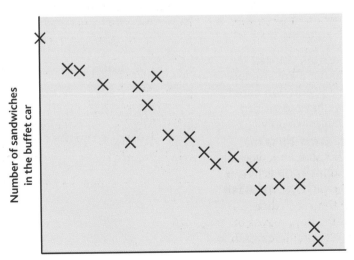

Number of passengers on the train

 C *Scatter graph showing negative correlation*

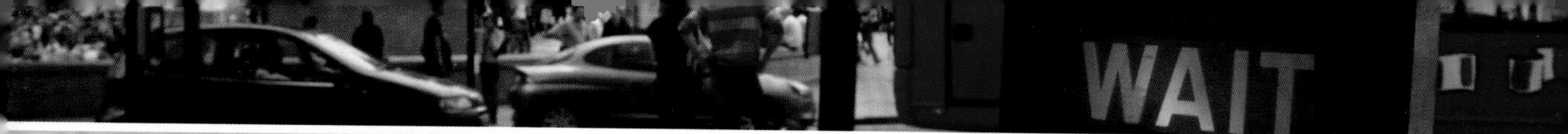

Starter activity

2 Look at the scatter graph you drew displaying your foot sizes and heights. Did you find a positive correlation? Most correlations for these two variables would usually result in a positive relationship. What does the relationship you found indicate about foot size and height in your group?

Key terms

Negative correlation: a relationship between two variables in which, as the value of one variable increases, the value of the other variable decreases.

No correlation: there is no relationship between the two variables.

Prediction: a statement about what will happen, made before the event occurs.

Negative correlation

Graph **C** shows a **negative correlation**. In a negative correlation, as the value of one variable increases, the value of the other variable decreases. The scatter graph shows how, as the number of passengers on a train increases, the number of sandwiches for sale in the buffet car at the end of a journey decreases.

No correlation

Graph **D** shows **no correlation** between the number of pets owned and the score in a maths test.

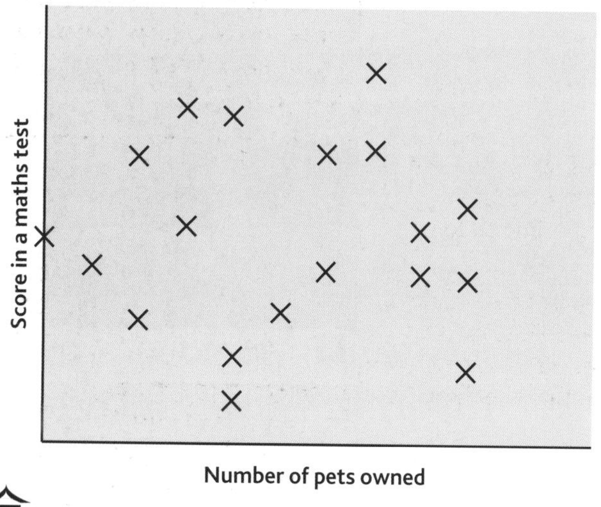

D *Scatter graph showing no correlation*

Did you know ??????

Marion Janner, in her Star Wards project (2006), discovered that pets like hamsters, snakes and rats kept in rooms by hospital wards reduced stress levels in patients. One nurse said, 'The patients would stroke the pet and their anxiety would go away.'

The more pets people have, the less stress they feel – a negative correlation that pet owners often remark on to those who do not have pets!

If you look at the scatter graph in Graph **A** on page 159, you can see that when there are lots of umbrellas being carried there are also lots of puddles on the ground. This allows us to make a **prediction** based on the type of correlation we have found. When we have identified a particular kind of relationship between two variables we only need to measure one of the variables to predict or 'guess' the likely measurement of the second variable. We can predict that on a day when there are lots of umbrellas being carried there *will also be* lots of puddles on the ground. What we *cannot* say is that carrying umbrellas *causes* puddles on the ground.

The only method that can establish a cause and effect relationship is an experiment. This is because the experimental method controls the extraneous variables that could also be causes. In a study where the variables are just measured it may be something else that has caused the positive relationship, such as between the number of umbrellas being carried and the number of puddles. In this particular example, this may well be the fact that it is raining!

Activity

2 Correlations are quite easy to carry out because researchers only need to measure variables and plot a scatter graph to see if the variables are related. Can you think of the advantages of correlations? What about the limitations of collecting and analysing data in this way?

Draw a chart with two columns. Head one column 'Advantages of correlations' and the other 'Limitations of correlations'. Discuss your ideas in a small group and try to complete the chart. Do not read on until you have completed this task.

Advantages and limitations of correlations

Correlation is a very useful technique for research in psychology. Here are some of the advantages:

- Correlation allows a researcher to see if two variables are connected in some way. This means that once a relationship has been found the researcher can use a different method, like an experiment, to try to find the cause of the results.

- Correlation can be used when it would be impossible or unethical to carry out an experiment. Researchers cannot force people to smoke in order to see if they then develop lung cancer. However, plotting the rates of smoking against lung cancer does tell us that they are related. This knowledge can influence behaviour.

There are also limitations to the use of correlations:

- Correlations do not indicate which of the two variables caused the relationship to occur. It is sometimes the case that other variables are the cause of the pattern seen on a scatter graph.

- In order for a correlation to be informative, there does need to be a large amount of data for each variable so that the possible pattern can be seen. This means the researcher needs to take lots of measurements of both variables so that the pattern in the data can be seen.

Check your understanding

1 What is meant by the term 'positive correlation'? *(2 marks)*

2 Explain why correlation can be useful in psychology. *(2 marks)*

3 What is the difference between an experiment and a correlation study? *(2 marks)*

AQA Examiner's tip

Remember, the heading for a scatter graph must always use the term 'relationship between …' rather than 'the effect of …' Do not write a heading that seems to suggest one variable has caused the other. Also, do not write your title as a question such as 'Is height related to foot size?' Once the graph has been drawn, you know what the relationship is: positive correlation, negative correlation or no correlation. You should use one of these phrases in your title.

Going further

You might like to see if you can find some examples of research that has used correlation. To get you started you could look up the work of B.I. Murstein (1972) on attractiveness and marital choice. Another study investigated the relationship between eye movements and dreaming – see W. Dement and M. Kleitman (1957). Much research into disorders like schizophrenia and depression has used correlated data. Use websites and textbooks to help you.

Present your findings to the rest of your group.

Key points to structure revision

1 Memory

Can you define these terms?

- Encoding
- Storage
- Retrieval
- Eyewitness testimony

 Examiner's tip When defining a term, for each extra mark you should add a new point in your answer.

Do you know the main features of these explanations of memory?

- Multi-store
- Reconstructive
- Levels of processing

Can you describe and evaluate studies to investigate these explanations of memory?

 Examiner's tip When you describe a study, remember to state the aim, method, results and conclusion.

Can you state **at least two** factors affecting the reliability of eyewitness testimony?

 Examiner's tip An examination question will never ask you to recall more than two factors.

Can you describe and evaluate studies that investigated each of these factors?

 Examiner's tip You do not need to remember dates of studies and if you forget the psychologist's name you won't lose marks.

Can you explain **at least two** practical applications coming from explanations of memory and forgetting? What are their benefits and drawbacks?

 Examiner's tip For an **application**, think about how can we put the knowledge gained from these explanations into practice in the real world?

2 Non-verbal communication

Can you distinguish between the following terms?

- Non-verbal communication
- Verbal communication
- Paralinguistics

 Examiner's tip When distinguishing between terms, use examples to help explain each term.

Can you describe and evaluate studies of non-verbal communication and verbal communication? The types of non-verbal communication you need to know are:

- functions of eye contact and pupil dilation
- categories of facial expression
- facial expressions and hemispheres of the brain
- body language: posture (including posture echo, open and closed postures), gesture and touch.

 Examiner's tip Remember that evaluations can be positive, negative or a combination of both.

Can you identify **at least two** factors that affect personal space? Can you describe and evaluate studies that investigated each of these factors?

Can you explain **at least two** practical implications of studies of non-verbal communication? What are their benefits and drawbacks?

 Examiner's tip For an **implication**, think about what these studies tell us about behaviour that is actually happening in the real world.

3 Development of personality

Can you define these terms?

- Personality
- Temperament

 AQA Examiner's tip When defining a term, do not use the term from the question in your answer.

Can you describe and evaluate studies of temperament, including the work of the following?

- Thomas
- Buss and Plomin
- Kagan and Snidman

 AQA Examiner's tip When you describe a study, remember to state the aim, method, results and conclusion. In your evaluation you can list three separate points or describe one point in detail.

Can you describe and evaluate Eysenck's type theory? This includes:

- extroversion
- introversion
- neuroticism
- personality scales – EPI, EPQ.

Can you state **at least two** characteristics of Antisocial Personality Disorder (APD)?

 AQA Examiner's tip An examination question will never ask you to recall more than two characteristics.

Can you describe causes of APD?

- Biological – the role of the amygdala
- Situational

 AQA Examiner's tip You may need to label the amygdala on a diagram of the brain.

Can you describe and evaluate studies that investigated each of these theories?

- Biological – Raine
- Situational – Farrington, Elander

 AQA Examiner's tip If you are asked to describe a study, you do not need to evaluate it.

Can you explain **at least two** implications of research into APD?

4 Stereotyping, prejudice and discrimination

Can you define these terms?

- Stereotyping
- Prejudice
- Discrimination

 AQA Examiner's tip When defining a term, for each extra mark you should add a new point in your answer.

Can you explain **at least one** advantage and **at least one** disadvantage of stereotyping?

Can you describe the following studies of prejudice and discrimination?

- Adorno and the authoritarian personality (including the F-scale)
- Tajfel and his theory of in-groups and out-groups
- Sherif and his theory of conflict between groups (Robbers Cave)

 AQA Examiner's tip When asked to describe a study in the exam, you may be asked for: the reason why the study was conducted (the aim), the method used, the results obtained and the conclusion drawn, or you may be asked for a combination of these components.

Can you evaluate the above-named studies?

Can you describe ways of reducing prejudice and discrimination using evidence from studies including the work of the following:

- Sherif
- Aronson
- Elliott
- Harwood

 AQA Examiner's tip You do not need to remember the dates of studies.

Can you evaluate the above ways of reducing prejudice and discrimination?

 AQA Examiner's tip Remember that evaluations can be positive, negative or both.

Can you explain **at least two** practical implications of research into stereotyping, prejudice and discrimination? What are their benefits and drawbacks?

5 Research methods

Can you explain these terms?

- Ecological validity
- Hypothesis
- Independent variable
- Dependent variable
- Extraneous variable
- Random allocation
- Counterbalancing
- Randomisation
- Target population

 AQA Examiner's tip When explaining a term, it is sometimes easier to use an example to help you to express your answer.

Do you know the main advantages and disadvantages of the following experimental designs?

- Independent groups
- Repeated measures
- Matched pairs

 AQA Examiner's tip Try to make sure that the advantages and disadvantages you discuss are relevant to the study that has been described, if the question requires that.

Do you know the main advantages and limitations of the following sampling methods?

- Random sampling
- Opportunity sampling
- Systematic sampling
- Stratified sampling

 AQA Examiner's tip Try to make your answers practical when you describe the advantages and limitations.

Can you calculate the following statistics?

- Mean
- Median
- Mode
- Range
- Percentages

 AQA Examiner's tip Remember to take your calculator into the examination with you! Be ready to spot **anomalous data** when you look at sets of scores and consider the possible effects of this on the mean in particular.

Can you draw and label graphs, especially bar charts?

 AQA Examiner's tip Make sure you do not plot individual scores of participants on the x-axis when you draw a graph.

Can you discuss advantages and limitations of research in natural and experimental settings?

 AQA Examiner's tip Think of good examples of each type of research from the topics you have studied. These will highlight the advantages and limitations.

Can you describe and discuss ethical issues in psychological research?

 AQA Examiner's tip You must be able to think of sensible ways of dealing with these issues.

Learning

Can you describe what is meant by the following terms used in classical conditioning?

- Unconditioned stimulus
- Unconditioned response
- Conditioned stimulus
- Conditioned response
- Extinction
- Spontaneous recovery
- Generalisation
- Discrimination

 You must be able to complete the classical conditioning schedule that uses the first four terms listed here, to show how learning can take place.

Can you discuss the contributions of Pavlov to our understanding of the learning process?

 Remember, contributions should include positive points as well as limitations.

Can you explain Thorndike's Law of Effect?

Can you discuss the contributions of Skinner to our understanding of the learning process?

Can you describe what is meant by the following terms used in operant conditioning and behaviour shaping?

- Positive reinforcement
- Negative reinforcement
- Punishment

 Remember to distinguish between reinforcement and punishment.

Can you describe and evaluate attempts to apply conditioning procedures to the following?

- The treatment of phobias, including flooding and systematic desensitisation
- Changing unwanted behaviour, including aversion therapy and the use of token economies

 Make sure that you can describe how the attempt works and the likely success of the method.

Can you discuss ethical issues that might occur in phobia treatments, aversion therapy and token economies?

 Social influence

Can you define these terms?

- Conformity
- Obedience
- Social loafing
- Deindividuation

 When defining a term, you need to make one point for each mark.

Can you describe and evaluate studies that have investigated conformity, obedience, social loafing and deindividuation?

 When evaluating a study, remember you can write about the method or the ethics.

Can you explain the factors that affect conformity, obedience, social loafing and deindividuation?

 Don't make the mistake of merely defining these terms when you are asked to explain factors that affect them.

Can you explain the factors that affect bystander intervention?

Can you describe and evaluate studies of bystander intervention, including those by the following?

- Latané and Darley
- Bateson
- Piliavin
- Schroeder

 Remember to include the reason for the study, the method, the results and the conclusion.

Can you explain **at least two** practical implications of studies of research into social influence? What are their benefits and their drawbacks?

 An **implication** of a study is an idea about what it tells us of similar behaviour beyond the research situation.

8 Sex and gender

Can you define and distinguish between the following terms?

- Sex identity
- Gender identity

AQA Examiner's tip When distinguishing between terms, use the word 'whereas' to show you are identifying the difference between them.

Can you identify these biological differences between males and females?

- Chromosomes
- Hormones

Can you describe these three theories of gender development?

- Psychodynamic theory – Oedipus and Electra complexes
- Social learning theory – imitation, modelling and vicarious reinforcement
- Gender schema theory

Can you evaluate these three theories?

- Psychodynamic theory – Oedipus and Electra complexes
- Social learning theory – imitation, modelling and vicarious reinforcement
- Gender schema theory

9 Aggression

Do you know the main features of these explanations of aggression?

- Biological, including the role of hormones, brain disease, and chromosomal abnormality
- Psychodynamic, including the frustration–aggression hypothesis
- Social learning, including modelling, punishment and monitoring

AQA Examiner's tip This requires an understanding of theories, not studies. The next section requires an understanding of studies not theories. It is important to understand the difference between these two terms.

Can you describe and evaluate studies of the development of aggression? This should include studies based on the following approaches:

- biological
- psychodynamic
- social learning

AQA Examiner's tip Remember, when evaluating studies, you can make positive as well as negative comments.

Can you describe ways of reducing aggression, based on these explanations?

- Biological
- Psychodynamic
- Social learning

AQA Examiner's tip Remember, the methods you describe must relate to the explanation named in the question.

Can you evaluate the ways of reducing aggression based on these explanations?

- Biological
- Psychodynamic
- Social learning

AQA Examiner's tip You can suggest why these ways are successful or unsuccessful.

Further research methods

Note: some of the material covered in **Chapter 5** is also needed here. This includes:

- target populations
- random sampling
- opportunity sampling
- systematic sampling
- stratified sampling.

Also, you may be required to deal with calculations of the following:

- mean
- median
- mode
- range
- percentages.

You need to be able to understand **anomalous results** and their possible effects. In the examination, you may be required to produce **graphical representations**, including bar charts. You must also be able to describe and discuss **ethical issues** and ways of dealing with these.

Can you describe and discuss the key features of survey methods, including questionnaires and interviews?

- Questionnaires – you must be able to distinguish between open and closed questions.
- Interviews – you must be able to distinguish between structured and unstructured interviews.

Can you describe and discuss the key features of the observation method, including what is meant by categories of behaviour and inter-observer reliability?

Can you describe and discuss case studies?

 Make sure that you can think of examples to illustrate each of the terms listed here.

Can you explain what is meant by the technique of 'correlation'?

 You need to be able to discuss the advantages and disadvantages or limitations of questionnaires, observation studies, case studies and correlation studies.

Glossary

Aggression: behaviour aimed at harming others.

Altruism: helping someone without thought of yourself, sometimes at great cost.

Amygdala: part of the brain involved in emotion.

Anomalous result: an extremely high or low result that does not match the other results in a set of scores.

Anonymous: being able to keep our identity hidden.

Anterograde amnesia: being unable to learn new information after suffering brain damage.

Antisocial Personality Disorder (APD): a condition in which the individual does not use socially acceptable behaviour or consider the rights of others.

Attention Deficit Hyperactivity Disorder (ADHD): a disorder characterised by short attention span, poor concentration and uncontrollable aggressive outbursts.

Authoritarian personality: a personality type that is prone to being prejudiced.

Autokinetic effect: an optical illusion, in which a spot of light on a screen appears to move, when in actual fact it doesn't.

Aversion therapy: a treatment for addictions, such as drug and alcohol dependency, which makes the addict have an extremely negative reaction to the addictive substance.

B

Behaviour shaping: changing behaviour in small steps.

'Bobo' doll: an inflatable doll of about 1.5 metres tall that is weighted at the bottom. It is designed to jump back up when it is knocked over.

Body language: a general term to describe aspects of non–verbal communication.

Brain disease: damage to the brain caused by illness or trauma.

British Psychological Society (BPS) Guidelines: the ethical guidelines produced by the British Psychological Society in its *Code of Ethics and Conduct* (2006) that govern the work of all practising and research psychologists and also of psychology students in the UK.

Buffer: something that creates distance between the teacher and learner (e.g. a wall or another person administering the shocks).

Bystander apathy: doing nothing in an emergency when someone is in need of help.

C

Case study: an in–depth investigation of an individual, a small group or an organisation.

Categories of behaviour: the separate actions that are recorded as examples of the target behaviour.

Catharsis: the process of getting rid of your emotions by watching other people experiencing emotion.

Chromosomes: the parts of each cell that carry the genetic information from our parents.

Classical conditioning: a procedure during which an animal or person learns to associate a reflex response with a new stimulus.

Classical conditioning schedule: the steps in the procedure to condition a new response.

Closed–circuit television (CCTV): a television system often used for surveillance.

Closed posture: positioning the arms so that they are folded across the body and/or crossing the legs.

Closed question: a question where the possible responses are fixed, often as 'yes' or 'no' options.

Cognitive interview: a method of questioning witnesses that involves recreating the context of an event.

Communication: passing information from one person to another.

Condition: an experiment is usually organised so there are two trials, after which the performances of the participants are compared. These are the conditions of the experiment.

Conditioned response (CR): the response that is learnt; it now occurs when the CS is presented, such as Pavlov's dog's salivation.

Conditioned stimulus (CS): a new stimulus presented with the UCS, such as the bell in Pavlov's experiment.

Confederate: an actor or stooge who appears to be a genuine participant in the experiment but is actually working for the experimenter.

Conformity: a change in a person's behaviour or opinions as the result of group pressure.

Contact: seeing, speaking or writing to someone.

Context: the general setting or environment in which activities happen.

Control: making sure procedures are the same when necessary. Not controlling procedures leads to the possibility of extraneous variables occurring and confounding the results.

Correlation: a technique used by researchers to establish the strength of a relationship between two variables.

Counterbalancing: a procedure for evening out the order in which participants complete both conditions of an experiment.

Cultural norms: the range of behaviours that members of a particular social group or society can be expected to show.

Culture: a group of people (usually living in one place) who share similar customs, beliefs and behaviour.

Curvilinear: a relationship that increases in strength to a point, but then begins to decrease.

D

Deindividuation: the state of losing our sense of individuality and becoming less aware of our own responsibility for our actions.

Dependent variable (DV): the variable that the researcher measures to see if the IV has affected it.

Diffusion of responsibility: in a group of people there is less need for the individual to act because someone else who is present could also do something.

Discrimination: (with reference to conditioning) the conditioned response is only produced when a specific stimulus is presented.

Discrimination: (with reference to prejudice) the way an individual behaves towards another person or group as a result of their prejudiced view. This behaviour is usually negative but could also be positive.

Displacement: being aggressive towards other people.

Dizygotic twins: twins developed from two separately fertilised eggs.

DSM–IV TR: lists different mental disorders and the criteria for diagnosing them.

E

Ecological validity: the results of the investigation can be said to apply to real–life behaviour.

They are an accurate account of behaviour in the real world.

Ego defence mechanisms: behaviour strategies used by the individual to protect itself.

Electra complex: the conflict experienced by a girl because she unconsciously desires her father and is afraid of losing her mother's love.

Empathy: being able to put yourself in someone else's position psychologically and understand how that person is feeling.

Emphasis: giving prominence to some words more than others.

Encoding: changing information so that it can be stored.

Ethical issues: points of concern about what is morally right.

Experiment: the method of research in which all variables other than the independent variable (IV) and dependent variable (DV) are controlled. This allows the researcher to identify a cause–and–effect relationship between the IV and DV.

Expert groups: another name for the jigsaw method. It is called expert groups because each member of the group becomes an expert on a particular topic and they then pass this knowledge on to the rest of their group.

Extinction: a conditioned response dies out.

Extraneous variable (EV): a variable that is not the IV but might affect the DV if it is not controlled.

Extroversion: a personality type that describes people who look to the outside world for entertainment.

Eye contact: when two people in conversation are looking at each other's eyes at the same time.

F

Flooding: a treatment for phobias that involves the immediate exposure of the person to the feared object, activity or event until there is no fear response.

F–scale: the questionnaire used by Adorno to measure personality characteristics.

G

Gender disturbance: not developing the gender identity usually associated with one's sex.

Gender identity: a psychological term. A child's gender can be identified by their attitudes and behaviour. This determines whether the child's gender identity is masculine or feminine.

Gender role: behaviour seen as masculine or feminine by a particular culture.

Gender schema: a mental building block of knowledge that contains information about each gender.

Gender stereotype: believing that all males are similar and all females are similar.

Generalisation: the conditioned response is produced when a similar stimulus to the original conditioned stimulus is presented.

Generalised: the results from the sample can be said to apply to the target population.

Gesture: a form of non–verbal communication in which information is conveyed by either deliberate or unconscious movement of parts of the body.

Grey matter (cerebral cortex): the outer layer of the brain.

H

Hemispheres of the brain: the human brain is divided into two halves, called the left and right hemispheres.

Hierarchy of fears: a series of feared events ranked from least frightening to most frightening.

Highly gender schematised: where gender is an important way of thinking about the world so information is organised according to what is gender appropriate and what is gender inappropriate.

Hippocampus: a brain structure that is crucial for memory.

Hormones: chemicals released by our endocrine system that affect how our bodies function and how we behave.

Hypothesis: a testable statement about the relationship between two variables. In an experiment these variables are called the independent variable (IV) and the dependent variable (DV).

I

Identification: to adopt the attitudes and behaviour of the same–sex parent.

Imitation: copying the behaviour of a model.

Independent variable (IV): the variable that the researcher alters or manipulates to look for an effect on another variable. This variable produces the two conditions of the study.

Individual differences: factors that make one person not the same as another person, such as personality or age.

In–group: a group of people you believe you have something in common with, for example, your psychology group.

Instructions: the written (or verbal) information given to participants during the experiment.

Interference: things that we have learnt that make it difficult to recall other information that we have learnt.

Inter–observer reliability: when this is high, the records made by more than one observer in a study are considered to be accurate because they match or are very similar to each other.

Interview: a method in which a researcher collects data by asking questions directly.

Interviewee: the person/respondent who answers the questions in an interview.

Intonation: inflection in the voice when speaking.

Introversion: a personality type that describes people who are content with their own company.

J

Jigsaw method: the name given to the technique used by Aronson to reduce prejudice within a group of mixed–race students.

L

Law of Effect: behaviours that are followed by rewards are usually repeated; those that are punished are not usually repeated.

Leading question: a question that hints that a particular type of answer is required.

Learning: a relatively permanent change in behaviour due to experience.

Levels of processing: the depth at which information is thought about when trying to learn it.

Limbic system: the part of the brain that causes aggressive behaviour.

Longitudinal study: a study carried out to show how behaviour changes over time.

Long–term store: holds a vast amount of information for a very long period of time.

M

Mean: a statistic calculated by adding all the scores in a set of values and dividing the total by the number of values in the set.

Media: means of communication – television, radio, the internet and newspapers are all examples of different types of media.

Median: the middle value in a set of values when the values have been arranged in ascending order.

Mode: the most frequently occurring value in a set of values.

Modelling: a role model provides an example for the child.

Monitoring: judging whether our own behaviour is appropriate or not.

Monozygotic twins: twins developed from one fertilised egg.

Multi–store: The idea that information passes through a series of memory stores.

Mundane realism: an everyday situation, that is life–like and not artificial.

N

Natural observation: watching the behaviour of people who are in their usual environment.

Negative correlation: a relationship between two variables in which, as the value of one variable increases, the value of the other variable decreases.

Negative reinforcement: when an unpleasant experience is removed after a behaviour or action has been made. This increases the likelihood of that behaviour or action being repeated.

Neuroticism: a personality type that describes people who are highly emotional and show a quick, intense reaction to fear.

No correlation: there is no relationship between the two variables.

Non–verbal communication: conveying messages that do not require the use of words or vocal sounds.

O

Obedience: following the orders of someone we believe to have authority.

Objectivity: not affected by personal biases.

Observation study: a method of collecting information about behaviour by watching and recording people's actions.

Oedipus complex: the conflict experienced by a boy in the phallic stage because he unconsciously desires his mother and is afraid of his father.

Open posture: positioning the arms so they are not folded across the body and not crossing the legs.

Open question: a question where the person answering can give any response they like.

Operant conditioning: learning due to the consequences of behaviour, through positive reinforcement or negative reinforcement.

Opportunity sample: people who are members of the target population and are available and willing to take part.

Order effect: this occurs when a participant's performance in the second condition of an experiment is affected because they have already done the first condition. They may do better because of practice or worse because of tiredness. This may happen in a repeated measures design.

Out–group: a group of people whom you believe you have nothing in common with.

P

Paralinguistics: vocal features that accompany speech.

Participant: a person who is selected to take part in a study.

Participant variables: the differences between the people who take part in the study. These may affect the results of an experiment that uses an independent groups design.

Percentage: a proportion expressed as a fraction of 100.

Personal space: the distance we keep between ourselves and other people in our everyday lives.

Personality: the thoughts, feelings and behaviours that make an individual unique.

Personality scales: ways of measuring personality using yes/no questions.

PET scan: a technique to show how the brain is working by imaging it while the patient is carrying out a mental task.

Phallic stage: Freud's third stage of psychosexual development, in which gender development takes place.

Phobia: a persistent and irrational fear of an object, activity or situation. The typical symptoms are intense feelings of fear and anxiety to avoid the object, activity or situation.

Phonetic processing: thinking about the sound of words to be learnt.

Positive correlation: a relationship between two variables in which, as the value of one variable increases, the value of the other variable also increases.

Positive reinforcement: a reward or pleasant consequence that increases the likelihood that a behaviour or action will be repeated.

Postural echo: mirroring another person's body position.

Posture: the positioning of the body, often regarded as a non–verbal communication signal.

Practical implications: suggestions about behaviour in the real world beyond the research study, based upon what psychologists have discovered.

Prediction: a statement about what will happen, made before the event occurs.

Prefrontal cortex: the very front of the brain. It is involved in social and moral behaviour and controls aggression.

Prejudice: a rigid set of attitudes or beliefs towards particular groups of people. These attitudes are usually negative, but not always.

Primacy effect: the first information received is recalled better than subsequent information.

Primary reinforcer: a reward, such as food or water, that the animal or person needs in order to survive.

Proactive interference: when information we have already learnt hinders our ability to recall new information.

Psychosurgery: an operation on the brain to remove or destroy the part that is causing abnormal behaviour.

Pyschoticism: a third dimension identified by Eysenck. People who score high on this dimension are hostile, aggressive, insensitive and cruel.

Punishment: a stimulus that weakens behaviour because it is unpleasant and we try to avoid it.

Pupil dilation: when the pupils in the eyes expand to look large.

Q

Questionnaire: a set of standard questions about a topic that is given to all the participants in the survey.

R

Random allocation: a procedure for putting participants into conditions by chance.

Randomisation: using chance to produce an order for a procedure.

Random sample: every member of the target population has an equal chance of being selected for the sample.

Range: the difference between the lowest and highest value in a set of values.

Raw data: the scores collected in a study that have not been analysed or summarised.

Recency effect: information received later is recalled better than earlier information.

Reconstructive memory: altering our recollection of things so that they make more sense to us.

Reinforcement: a consequence of behaviour that encourages or strengthens a behaviour. This might be seen as a reward.

Relationship: a connection between two or more variables.

Reliability: in the context of eyewitness testimony, the extent to which it can be regarded as accurate.

Representative: the sample of participants is made up of people who have the same characteristics and abilities as the target population.

Repress: keep our emotions under very tight control and not express how we are feeling.

Respondents: the people who take part in a survey.

Retrieval: recovering information from storage.

Retroactive interference: when information we have recently learnt hinders our ability to recall information we have learnt previously.

Retrograde amnesia: loss of memory for events that happened before brain damage occurred.

Ritalin: a drug used to control Attention Deficit Hyperactivity Disorder (ADHD).

Robbers Cave: the name given to Sherif's experiment on prejudice.

Role model: someone who a child looks up to and is likely to copy.

S

Sample: the small group of people who represent the target population and who are studied.

Scatter graph: a graph for representing correlations.

Secondary reinforcer: a reward, such as money or a token, that the animal or person can exchange for a primary reinforcer.

Semantic processing: thinking about the meaning of words to be learnt.

Sensory store: holds information received from the senses for a very short period of time.

Sex differences: differences due to being either male or female; these could affect personal space between individuals.

Sex identity: a biological term. A child's sex can be identified by their hormones and chromosomes. This determines whether the child's sex identity is male or female.

Short–term store: holds approximately seven chunks of information for a limited amount of time.

Social influence: the effect other people have on our behaviour. This includes conformity, obedience and social loafing, for example.

Socialisation: the way we are raised to behave and the things we are taught to accept as normal.

Social loafing: putting less effort into doing something when you are with others doing the same thing.

Socioeconomic factors: social and financial issues that can affect an individual.

Spontaneous recovery: a conditioned response that has disappeared suddenly appears again.

Standardised procedures: a set order of carrying out a study that is applied to all participants when necessary.

Status: a person's rank or position within society.

Stereotype: an oversimplified, generalised set of ideas that we have about others, for example, secondary head teachers are strict, intimidating, scary and male.

Storage: holding information in the memory system.

Stratified sample: to obtain this type of sample, the different subgroups in the target population are identified; then people are randomly selected from these subgroups in proportion to their numbers in the target population.

Structural processing: thinking about the physical appearance of words to be learnt.

Structured interview: an interview in which all the questions are pre–set, given in a fixed order and every interviewee is asked the same questions.

Sublimation: channelling our aggression into other acceptable activities.

Survey: a method used for collecting information from a large number of people by asking them questions, either by using a questionnaire or in an interview.

Systematic desensitisation: a treatment for phobias in which the person is taught to relax and then is gradually exposed to the feared object, activity or event.

Systematic sample: every 'nth' member of the target population is selected for the sample.

T

Target population: the large group of people the researcher wishes to study.

Temperament: the genetic component of personality.

Thanatos: the part of our unconscious that causes our aggressive drive.

Tone of voice: the way words are spoken to convey emotion.

Touch: a form of non–verbal communication in which information is conveyed by physical contact between people.

Type theory: personality types are thought to be inherited. They can be described using related traits.

U

Unambiguous: something that has only one meaning.

Unconditioned response (UCR): the reflex response to an unconditioned stimulus, such as Pavlov's dog's salivation.

Unconditioned stimulus (UCS): the stimulus that produces a reflex response, such as the food for Pavlov's dog.

Unstructured interview: an interview in which only the first question is set and all other questions are determined by the answers of the interviewee.

Variable: a factor or thing that can change – it varies.

Verbal communication: conveying messages using words or vocal sounds.

Vicarious learning: learning by observation.

Vicarious reinforcement: learning from the model's being either rewarded or punished.

Index